T0289784

ROUTLEDGE LIBRARY EDITIONS:
THE ECONOMICS AND BUSINESS OF
TECHNOLOGY

Volume 14

FEDERAL INFLUENCES ON BIOMEDICAL TECHNOLOGY INNOVATION

FEDERAL INFLUENCES ON BIOMEDICAL TECHNOLOGY INNOVATION

LILLY B. GARDNER

Routledge
Taylor & Francis Group

LONDON AND NEW YORK

First published in 1994 by Garland Publishing Inc

This edition first published in 2018
by Routledge
2 Park Square, Milton Park, Abingdon, Oxon OX14 4RN

and by Routledge
711 Third Avenue, New York, NY 10017

Routledge is an imprint of the Taylor & Francis Group, an informa business

British Library Cataloguing in Publication Data
A catalogue record for this book is available from the British Library

ISBN: 978-1-138-50336-6 (Set)
ISBN: 978-1-351-06690-7 (Set) (ebk)
ISBN: 978-0-8153-6265-4 (Volume 14) (hbk)
ISBN: 978-1-351-11143-0 (Volume 14) (ebk)

Publisher's Note
The publisher has gone to great lengths to ensure the quality of this reprint but
points out that some imperfections in the original copies may be apparent.

Disclaimer
The publisher has made every effort to trace copyright holders and would welcome
correspondence from those they have been unable to trace.

FEDERAL INFLUENCES ON BIOMEDICAL TECHNOLOGY INNOVATION

LILLY B. GARDNER

GARLAND PUBLISHING, INC.
NEW YORK & LONDON / 1994

Library of Congress Cataloging-in-Publication Data

Gardner, Lilly B., 1935–
    Federal influences on biomedical technology innovation / Lilly B.
Gardner.
        p.   cm. — (Garland studies on the elderly in America : [   ])
    Includes bibliographical references and index.
    ISBN 0–8153–1578–3
    1. Medical innovations—Government policy—United States.
2. Intervention (Federal government)—United States.   3. Medicine—
Research—Government policy—United States.   I. Title. II. Series.
R855.5.U6G37   1994
362.1'072073—dc20   93–37596
                                                                                    CIP

Printed on acid-free, 250-year-life paper
Manufactured in the United States of America

Contents

Preface

Health policy and service are generally matters of concern to all individuals, as they are intimately related to life and well-being. They are a focus of continual discussion and debate regarding how they should be organized, financed, and delivered. In a discussion of policy concerns pertaining to the posture of government in personal health services, S. C. Jain has suggested that the role of the government in the field of health mirrors the history of the overall role of the government in the United States (1983). The basic concerns of health policy have been the same as for overall social policy; their direction guided by similar values, events and development.

There is also a close relationship among society, technological development and government. Social values, institutions and political structures shape both the development and adoption of many technologies; conversely, technology provides the driving force behind many social changes. Governments have always strongly influenced trends in technological development, either indirectly through subsidies, tax incentives, pricing policies, and support for sectors including health care, or directly through research and development and actual purchases of new technologies (Teich, 1981).

Throughout the early years of United States history, the government's influence in medical technology development was marginal; during the middle years, governmental intervention rose steadily with the primary initiative for developing and delivering services left to the state and local governments (Jain, 1983). In the 1960s, through an increasing action posture on the part of Congress in health matters, the federal government rapidly expanded its involvement in biomedical research. This growing government involvement contributed both to the rapid development of medical technology and escalating health care costs (Gibson & Waldo, 1981).

The process by which new technology proceeds from the conception of a new idea (as a means of solving a problem) to the solution of a problem, and the subsequent utilization of the new item for economic gain or the advance of society is referred to as technological innovation. Technological innovation has been described as the nexus that joins science, technology, commerce and industry. It is both the sum and the result of a society producing social and economic impact on itself (Myers & Marquis, 1969).

Today, in the United States, health care provides numerous examples of the complexities inherent in the innovation process. For one, the American public has greatly benefitted from the government's strong support of the medical technological innovation process. This improvement has been demonstrated by increases in life expectancy, improvements in the quality of life, and ready access to quality health care (Comptroller General of the United States, 1985). These same technological breakthroughs have also greatly effected the economy by contributing both to the development of a major industry and to the escalation of health care delivery costs; biomedical research expenditures alone being in excess of $5.4 billion in 1986 (Califano, Jr.,1986). New diagnostic and treatment technologies, many of which benefit the elderly, such as computed axial tomographic (CAT) scanning, bypass surgery, renal dialysis and total hip replacement are examples of the dramatic manifestations of a technological knowledge base that now suffuses the health care system.

Medical technology has become a policy issue largely because of the rising costs of medical care (Banta, Burns & Behney, 1983). If we accept the fact that the health care budget is finite, then it follows that an explicit decision to allocate money for one set of services means that an implicit decision has also been made not to spend money on other services. In more specific terms, policy makers will need to decide if costly high-technology medical interventions for a few individuals should limit access to preventive care by large numbers of individuals.

For those technologies in which government is both the primary developer and user there is a continuous need to examine how society governs the emergence of the technology; that is, how does the government affect the cycle from research to development, to demonstration, to operations, and who influences government policy along the way. The rapid growth of government subsidized health delivery services further underscores the need to address a number of important policy questions. Among these are questions related to the understanding of the relationship between R&D, technological innovation, technological progress and economic growth, on the one hand, and between government, industry and university on the other.

This book examines a small segment of the medical technology innovation process to characterize the manner in which the federal government influences small business-based investigators to participate or withdraw from the medical technology innovation process. Through the consideration of the incentives and disincentives to participate, it was believed it would be possible to describe some of the ramifications of the federal government's ad hoc approach to the formulation of technology policy.

OVERVIEW OF THE CONTENTS

Chapters I through IV provide a pertinent historical account of the federal government's involvement in biomedical technology research and development, and traces the social and economic significance of this involvement. Chapter V discusses the role of the researcher in the biomedical technology innovation process; with special attention being given to rights in data, copyright and patent rights, and funding options available to this type of entrepreneur.

Chapter VI describes the methods used to identify conditions favoring innovations on the prevention side of the biomedical technology innovation process. Eight innovation proposals were prepared and submitted to the National Institutes of Health (NIH) through the Small Business Innovation Research Program (SBIR). Data about these National Cancer Institute (NCI) approved innovation demonstration projects were analyzed to develop an understanding of the manner in which the innovation process works in the NIH biomedical setting.

The eight proposals provided the basis for Chapter VII's characterization of the manner in which the government influences entrepreneurial researcher to participate or withdraw from the biomedical technology innovation process. By focusing on innovation at various levels of behavior--from creativity at the level of single individuals and decision making in small groups, to policy formation at the institutional level--it was believed it also would be possible to determine whether these incentives are sufficiently strong to move the process forward. The final chapter reflects on findings and proposes modifications to the NIH biomedical technology innovation process.

In 1992, this author once again received a grant under the SBIR program at the National Cancer Institute, NIH. The Phase I project was completed in the winter of 1992 and an application for a Phase II award was submitted. All indications point to a successful bid for this second phase award in late 1993 or early 1994. It is this author's hope that this book will provide encouragement for researchers with an entrepreneurial spirit to take the time to learn the system and actively take part in the biomedical technology innovation environment, for the rewards can be many.

Potomac, Maryland   Lilly B. Gardner
September, 1993

Federal Influences on Biomedical Technology Innovation

I

Health and Government

HISTORICAL OVERVIEW

In early United States history, the role of the government in health matters was quite minimal. Basic concerns of health policy closely followed the basic concerns of social policy and emphasized life, liberty and the pursuit of happiness. Personal health, illness, and disability were considered to be matters of individual concern and responsibility (Tesh, 1982); sanitation, care of indigent sick and quarantine laws were matters of governmental concern (Hanlon, 1974; Courtwright, 1980). Since the Constitution made no mention of health, Congress was considered to have little or no authority to act on health related matters.

Government influence in health continued to be marginal through the first half of the 19th Century despite the fact that the country generally experienced a great political and economic expansion. Initiatives at the federal level consisted of a number of failed quarantine control projects undertaken with the passage of a law in 1879, creating a National Board of Health. The board went out of business in 1884, when the authorizing legislation expired (Jain, 1983).

Then in 1886, a U.S. Supreme Court decision, which modified an earlier decision assigning basic quarantine authority to the states, provided the basis for an effective federal role in the health field. As a result of this ruling (*J.P. Morgan's Louisiana and Texas Railroad and Steamship Company v. Board of Health of Louisiana and State of Louisiana, cited in Jain, 1983*), what started out as a battle over authority for quarantine ended up in a steady and effective expansion

3

of federal involvement in health care (1983). Examples of this expansion included:

1. Establishment of a Federal research laboratory in 1887.
2. Organization of the Public Health and Marine Hospital Service in 1902.
3. Adoption of the Pure Food and Drug Act in 1906.
4. Establishment of the Children's Bureau in 1912.
5. Establishment of the National Leprosarium in 1917.
6. Establishment of the Division of Venereal Disease in the United States Public Health Service (USPHS) in 1918.

Even with this increased involvement, primary emphasis was placed on serving the health needs of the military and merchant seamen (1983). As late as 1935, federal funding for medical programs for the civilian population remained only a fraction of that expended by state and local governments.

S.C. Jain (1983), suggests that the adoption of the Social Security Act (Public Law [P.L.] 74-271, 1935) represents a major breakthrough in government involvement. Although this legislation did not provide for any revolutionary measures in the health field, it did set the tone for future authority in social welfare concerns. By establishing a number of principles of governmental responsibilities, this act set in motion many developments of far reaching consequences. Of special significance was the introduction of a principle of entitlement that placed an obligation on the federal government to provide certain services and payments to all eligible citizens without a means test. Even though the ground work had been laid for increased involvement, opposition to such activities was sufficiently strong to prevent any major initiatives except for those provided by the Social Security Amendments of 1950 (P. L. 81-734). These amendments sanctioned limited medical services to those on public assistance under a federal-state cost-sharing arrangement based on grants-in-aid.

The real shift in the role of the government came about in the 1960s, when policies and programs were initiated to assure "the highest level of health attainable for every person." The Social Security Amendments Act of 1965 (P. L. 89-97), better known as the Medicare-Medicaid Act, resulted in the strengthening of the federal role in two ways: The first was to establish a national level entitlement program, and the second--an unintended factor--was the unforeseen rapid rise in the costs of Medicare and Medicaid programs.

Congress continued to strongly support health initiatives through 1981, with each new piece of legislation directly or indirectly expanding and strengthening the federal presence. The redistributive and regulatory reforms brought about by these laws resulted in the federal government assuming a large share of the financial burden for both the provision of medical services and medical research (Starr, 1982). A large part of the growth in health care in recent years, has been due to the enormous quantity of resources spent in providing medical care. The rapid development of expensive medical technology has also created rapidly rising health costs.

Today, the federal involvement in health care is substantial and includes in its broad range of programs those designed to modulate the supply of physicians and hospitals, encourage the development of medical technology, expand care for the poor and elderly, and disseminate health information. The largest components of the federal effort are the Medicare and Medicaid programs that pay for services in the non-governmental sector either directly or through cost-sharing grants to the state agencies who pay for these services (Comptroller General of the United States, 1985); and the Public Health Service's National Institutes of Health, the principal federal medical research and development component (Jacoby, 1983).

In the thirty years that have passed since 1960, crude indicators of health show significant improvements. Infant mortality was cut in half (Bureau of the Census, 1981), life expectancy at birth increased by four years to more than age 74 (1981), death rates from cardiovascular diseases began to decline (Levy, 1981), and the major gaps between medical need and use of services by the poor and the old have diminished (Comptroller General of the United States, 1985).

The success of government programs designed to improve sanitation, develop effective vaccines, and provide for mass immunizations drastically shifted the pattern of killing and disabling diseases. Today, most of the communicable diseases have been brought under control. On the other hand, chronic diseases, such as heart disease, cancer and arthritis, have replaced communicable diseases as the major health problem in this country (Institute of Medicine, 1983). While many chronic diseases are not preventable, there are certain lifestyles changes which could possibly reduce the risk or delay the onset of these diseases. The unhealthy lifestyle issues were addressed at the federal level in 1979 (USPHS).

GOVERNMENT INTEREST IN DISEASE PREVENTION

In his 1979 report, the Surgeon General established broad National goals for improvement of the health of Americans at the five major life stages (USPHS, 1979). A year later, specific and measurable objectives were quantified and a request was made for a national commitment to reduce the rates of premature death and disability, (1980). That report concluded there was a need for better data to profile current status and to track progress toward the established objectives. To obtain valid results, test and control populations of considerable size would need long term follow-up, and a multiplicity of variables would need to be systematically taken into account. There would also be a need for basic biomedical, social and behavioral research in these prevention areas (1980).

PREVENTION ACTIVITIES

Currently, the government supports a broad range of preventive activities (Roemer, 1984). One key preventive service is immunization, delivered to individuals by physicians, nurses, other health professionals, and trained allied health workers. Also important are standards, voluntary agreements, laws and regulations such as engineering standards, safety regulations and toxic agent control, to protect people from hazards to health in their living, traveling and working environments. Financial support of prevention activities has been almost entirely directed toward providing funds to the states to work with local health departments and in promoting activities that individuals may adopt voluntarily to promote healthier habits of living,[1] or that employers and communities may adopt to encourage them.[2]

Relatively few prevention services such as routine physical examinations or Papanicalaou smears are classified as reimbursable under current Health Care Financing Administration (HCFA) or Civilian Health and Medical Program for the Uniformed Services (CHAMPUS) programs.

FUTURE TRENDS IN BIOMEDICAL TECHNOLOGY INNOVATION

As a supplement to the Arthur Anderson and Company and American College of Hospital Administrators' report dealing with health care in the future (1984), the Comptroller General's report suggested that the health care system in this country will most likely continue to encourage medical technological advances permitting earlier diagnosis and treatment of major illnesses (1985). Undoubtedly, the federal government will also be involved in shaping the future direction of the biomedical technology innovation process either directly through support and purchase of new technologies, or indirectly through reimbursement practices.

CHAPTER 1 NOTES

[1] Comptroller General's 1985 report listed unhealthy life styles such as alcohol and drug abuse smoking, obesity, lack of exercise, and improper diet as contributing to health problems (pp. 157-158).

[2] Ibid (pp. 172-177).

II

Federal Involvement

NATIONAL INSTITUTES OF HEALTH

In 1930, the Hygienic Laboratory, which was established in 1902 to test and improve biological products, was reorganized under the Ransdell Act to become the NIH. Since those humble beginnings, NIH has grown to be the principal medical research and development component of the federal government (Jacoby, 1983). As one of the five health agencies of the Public Health Service, NIH serves as a major resource for advancing biomedical and other health-related technologies. It also collaborates with other agencies, universities, industry, and state and local governments in both its research and its technology transfer activities.

In order to carry out its mandate to improve the health of the nation, NIH supports research in the biomedical sciences designed for acquisition of new knowledge to help prevent, detect, diagnose, and treat disease. Among its wide-ranging functions are the conduct and support of:

1. Research into the causes, prevention, and treatment of diseases.
2. Research training and development of research resources.
3. Assessment of the resulting information.
4. Information dissemination.

Assessment and transfer of information on health-related technologies are implemented by the Bureaus, Institutes, and Divisions (BID) of NIH and the Office of Medical Applications Research

9

(OMAR). OMAR was established in 1978, by the Assistant Secretary for Management and Budget to act as the focal point for activities aimed at improving the assessment and dissemination of results from NIH-supported biomedical research (USPHS, 1984). OMAR's functions include:

1. Advising the NIH Director and the BIDs on medical applications of research.
2. Coordinating, reviewing and facilitating the systematic identification and evaluation of clinically relevant NIH program information.
3. Promoting the effective transfer of such information to the health care community and other agencies requiring such information.
4. Providing a link between technology assessment activities for the BIDs and the Office of Health Technology Assessment, National Center for Health Science Research (NCHSR).
5. Monitoring the effectiveness and progress of NIH assessment and transfer activities.

As the Office of Research and Technology Applications (ORTA) for NIH, OMAR has a two-fold objective:

1. To conduct technology assessment and technology transfer programs such as consensus conferences, the review and analysis of issues related to HCFA policies on Medicare coverage of medical technology, and the NIH/Department of Health and Human Services (DHHS) Patent Program.
2. To conduct research and evaluation of technology assessment and transfer methods.

Just as the list of new health care technologies has constantly been growing, so also has NIH's involvement in assessing these technologies. When it deems appropriate, NIH actively promotes their wide-spread use.

Technology assessment and technology transfer are processes that include a series of events aimed at moving medical technologies from their creation to their application in clinical practice. The Stevenson-Wydler Technology Innovation Act of 1980, states as policy that federally funded technology should be utilized to the fullest extent and transferred where appropriate, to state and local governments and to the private sector (P.L. 96-480).

The Office of the Director, OMAR, NIH, describes technology innovation as a process including at least eight steps:

1. Discovery or basic research.
2. Development or applied research.
3. Evaluation or tests for safety and efficacy.
4. Assessment of potential value.
5. Demonstration or feasibility for widespread use.
6. Education.
7. Diffusion.
8. Broad application.

Once the assessment process indicates the safety and efficacy of a new technology, NIH, in selected circumstances, may elect to support further development and demonstrate potential for widespread application. In most cases, however, industry and the health professions are left to implement the technology transfer. This is in keeping with current science policy which focuses Federal R&D resources on basic research and leaves the support of technological development for purposes of commercialization (diffusion) in the hands of private industry.

Diffusion has two phases: the initial period during which the decision is made to adopt the innovation, and the subsequent and continuing period encompassing the decision to use the innovation. Research and policy have focused on adoption, with little available empirical research being done on the diffusion (Banta, Burns, & Behney, 1983). Additionally, little communication between researchers and practitioners takes place; limiting our ability to distinguish between successful and unsuccessful innovation (1983).

OMAR recognizes the existence of some relationship between adoption and use of a technology when it notes that Medicare reimbursement for the use of a given medical technology can serve as a strong facilitator of its adoption in general medical practice; reimbursement policies for Medicaid and private insurance plans often follow Medicare's lead (Office of Technology Assessment [OTA],

1984). They also state that, conversely, there is a strong barrier to adoption in the absence of Medicare reimbursement.

During Fiscal Years 1983 and 1984, OMAR was involved in over 70 HCFA Medicare coverage issues primarily involving medical/scientific considerations as to whether charges for a new or unusual item or service should be covered under Medicare as reasonable and necessary health care expenses.[1]

TRANSFORMING IDEAS INTO INNOVATIONS: SCIENCE POLICY IN THE U.S.

There are considerable differences in the process by which a technology enters and becomes part of the health care system. These differences are based on characteristics of the technology, complexity of understanding and using it, and observability or visibility of the results (Tanon & Rogers, 1975).

Setting Federal Priorities

Today, the U.S. technology policy is ad hoc in nature; consisting of innumerable laws, practices, and ingrained patterns with no overriding direction. The many separate parts may be productive for a narrow purpose, only to have a negative influence overall (Roe, 1987). As there also is no federal R&D budget per se, the allocation process for science and technology has tended to be largely incremental and segmented (Bartocha & Soloman, 1985).

The method most frequently used by policy makers and practitioners for broadly allocating resources in science has been of the task force/panel of experts/state-of-the-art review approach. One of the first and most notable examples of this approach is Bush's report, *Science-- The endless frontier* (cited in Bartocha & Soloman, 1985). While the report is not itself widely known, its legacy, the establishment of the National Science Foundation (NSF) closely resembles Bush's National Research Foundation.

Another example of the use of task force/panel of experts is exemplified by a series of federally sponsored surveys assessing the state of the art, needs, and plans undertaken by the National Academy of Science's Committee on Science and Public Policy from 1962 to 1974 (National Academy of Sciences, 1978). In a review of the utility of such surveys, William Lowrance (cited in Bartocha & Solomon, 1985) enumerated some of their inherent limitations. First, while scientists can be drafted to work with others in conducting surveys, they are reluctant to participate in what they view as their own execution. Secondly, surveys must unavoidably sacrifice some precision of analysis and impact because of their breadth of coverage. A third limitation is the lack of a "client-driven" orientation; i.e., the surveys have principally examined what was needed to advance the sciences themselves rather than looking at external or societal requirements.

As a tool devised by scientists and used by scientists, this egocentric orientation is appropriate, but as a mechanism to provide information to policy makers as part of their ongoing budget-making process to be used as an aid in setting scientific priorities, the orientation and content become more inadequate. (Bartocha & Solomon, 1985, p. 8).

An article entitled, "Peer Review and the Public Interest" (Atkinson & Blanpied, 1985), describes the unique relationship between science and government in the United States. In May 1950, the creation of NSF ended five years of negotiations between the scientific community and the government. This agreement was a political contract negotiated in the political arena, according to political rules, by a broad spectrum of skillful scientists. Its unique feature was the assumption that science would best serve the public interest if scientists, as private citizens, retained influence over how public funds were spent to support scientific activities. The integrity of peer review was considered essential to make this work.

Recent federal budget deficit reduction proposals designed to substantially reduce funding for domestic programs are directly challenging the old paradoxical claim that society will obtain maximum benefits from science if scientists are allowed to pursue their work free from interventions (Atkinson & Blanpied, 1985).

Given budgetary pressures, the Reagan Administration designed the following U.S. Science Policy:

1. To enhance the contributions of science to needs of national defense and the industrial competitiveness of U.S. industry.
2. To maximize the return of national R&D investments.
3. To ensure the long-term vitality of the U.S. science and technology base.

These translated into a U.S. Technology Policy objective ensuring that U.S. scientific leadership results in economic and defense leadership (Brown, 1985).

In order to accomplish this objective, policy makers attempt to direct the nation's scientific work in the most socially useful directions by regulating the choice of research topics. The mechanisms most frequently employed are Requests for Proposals (RFP) and Requests for Applications (RFA) (NIH, 1986, December). The RFP is designed to solicit bids from qualified profit-oriented and/or nonprofit organizations for a specific scope of work. The RFA is employed to encourage investigator-initiated research projects in areas of special interest to the government. Responsibility for planning, direction, and execution of the proposed research is solely that of the applicant.

There is no agreement as to whether governmental oversight in setting priorities is good or bad for science. There are those who argue that those scientific disciplines that have forged a consensus about their priorities have acquired the strength and cohesion required to negotiate with individual government agencies for the resources they need (Atkinson & Blanpied, 1985). While this trend is promising, it neither addresses the problem of the overall size of the federal R&D budget nor its distribution among agencies and programs.

The problem of establishing priorities across rather than within disciplines has yet to be clearly faced, although attempts in that direction have been made (1985). However, while mechanisms such as workshops and annual research briefings have been useful for information exchange and for helping the separate disciplines sort out their own priorities, there is no evidence that they have had any appreciable effect in determining resource allocation across disciplines or among agency programs.

It has been further argued that there is a larger problem of whether peer review can or should operate at an even higher level of aggregation to allocate resources among federal R&D agencies, or to even help determine the overall size of the federal R&D budget. The current environment suggests that the government does not view federal dollars for research as a right, but rather as a privilege to be subjected to the scrutiny of accountability and payoff.

By attempting to direct future scientific endeavors in the most socially useful directions, supporting agencies have offered scientists a mix of incentives and restrictions which displace the scientists' own professional judgments about what subjects to work on and how to proceed. Most importantly, scientists are encountering greater government regulation of the choice of research topics (Bartocha & Solomon, 1985).

Some scientists, reacting to these indirect federal controls, have attempted to take their claims directly to Congress, by retaining professional lobbying firms.[2] The fact that at least one spokesperson for the Office of Management and Budget (OMB) characterized scientists as "the quintessential special interest group"[3] is indicative of strains in the relationship between science and government.

Tactics which tamper with the "normal" appropriations process have been documented in the National Science Board's 1986 committee report. Referred to as pork barrel tactics, these activities are described as violations of the understanding that available resources are to be allocated in the best overall interests of science and the public-rather than in the interests of the individual claimants, no matter how deserving.

IMPORTANCE OF IMPROVED TECHNOLOGY MANAGEMENT

Science allocation issues highlight the complex interdependent relationship between the public--as represented by federal funding, and the scientific community--involving thousands of scientists, in the advance of the nation's biomedical research effort. Despite the difficulties in moving toward more appropriate use of medical technology, it is important that we do so, for several reasons.

While resources for health care were expanding, new programs could be added without upsetting the balance in other parts of the system. But now, with limited resources, the government cannot afford to continually expand services, nor can it afford to reduce one program without recognizing the impact of that decision on any one of several related, perhaps, more critical programs (Brook & Lohr, 1986). No matter how this country addresses the problems of the health care system, no program to arrange practical medical care for the nation can be implemented without science and technology as active catalysts and ingredients.

Serving the public interest in health planning must include not only prolonging the lives of diseased persons, but also attempting to understand why illnesses occur. Neither can we separate the scientific aspects of these issues from the social-economic-political ones for isolated analysis and decision.

CHAPTER II NOTES

[1]   Data provided by NIH, OMAR, DHHS, 1986.
[2]   One tactic includes use of last minute floor amendments to government funding bills, thereby circumventing project evaluation by responsible review groups.
[3]   In *Science and Government Report*, Daniel Green attributed this remark to an unidentified OMB official; George Keyworth II, President Reagan's Science Advisor quoted it in an address delivered at the AAAS colloquium on R&D in the Federal Budget, April 3, 1985. Cited in Atkinson & Blanpied, 1985.

III

Social Significance

OVERVIEW

Complex machines and devices now provide physicians with the technological means to diagnose illness and with facilities and specialists who operate and interpret the technology. These advances in medical skills and knowledge have not only affected the nature of medical services, their efficacy to alter suffering has greatly stimulated consumer demand (Banta, Burns & Behney, 1983).

The Comptroller General's 1985 report describes the health care consumer as one who generally believes that:

1. Medical care is a right and the entire population should have ready access to the health care system regardless of the nature of the illness or cost of treatment.
2. The medical care system can cure any illness.
3. The population should be protected from catastrophic financial loss because of medical problems and should be able to obtain medical care at little or no direct cost.

These consumer expectations have forced changes within the health care system which are both complex and far reaching. Four major changes in society appear to have the greatest impact on health care delivery. The first two deal with the increased demand for more and new services; the second two with pressure for change in how the services are ordered and financed.

1. Population Changes. A growing and aging population creates demand for both more services and different types of services.

Between the mid-1950s and the late 1960s, there was no significant increase in life expectancy for any group of Americans (National Center for Health Statistics, 1984). Since 1968, decreases in death rates have benefitted all age groups, with infants and those over 65 years of age benefiting most (Robert Wood Johnson Foundation, 1982). A growing percentage of our population over 65 visit doctors more often, experience longer hospital stays, and require over 20,000 nursing homes with 1.3 million beds (Comptroller General, 1985). The changing structure and functions of the American family, with more women working, make it less likely that the needs of the elderly will be met at home. One of the most difficult issues the expensive medical care of the aged raises, is how to allocate resources across the needs of the entire population in an equitable manner (Brook & Lohr, 1986).

2. Increased Purchasing Power. As the income of the average American rises so does his ability to turn more medical needs into market demand. This is most vividly illustrated through expanded workplace fringe benefits, which include better and more comprehensive medical benefits (Aaron & Schwartz, 1984).

3. Growing Popular Medical Sophistication. As the public becomes more aware of the benefits of good health practices and medical care, the demand for formerly unknown and unmet needs increases (American Medical Association [AMA], 1984). Problems of access inequalities in the kinds of care given, and new and better ways of organizing and financing care become public concerns. Society is becoming increasingly sophisticated about medicine, is better able to identify faulty aspects of the health care system and is becoming aware that the system is so diffuse no single means is available to change it (Lebow, 1974).

4. Egalitarian Ideology. The concept of equality of opportunity for access to employment, education, and the basic necessities of life has been expanded to include health care. Combined with the changes above, accelerating technological innovation, rapid specialization, and increasing centralization of care further increase both costs and demand on our health care system (Freund & Jellinek, 1983).

PUBLIC VIEWS REGARDING MEDICAL
TECHNOLOGY INNOVATION

In a recent analysis, the American public was found to be strongly supportive of science and technology and generally looks to science and technology to provide an improved quality of life. Results of a survey in 1983, by Louis Harris, found that the public was reluctant to impose restraints on scientific inquiry on most topics, and that the majority of Americans hold great expectations for science and technology in health related areas (cited in National Science Board, 1985). There also seems to be an assumption that the adoption of a new medical technology innovation is desirable even if it has not been shown to be an improvement of those currently in use. An OTA report suggests that the use of new technologies which are not improved technologies frequently spread rapidly as a result of media publicity (1982). Only later may the research assess their efficacy (Institute of Medicine, 1983).

Ever since financial constraint asserted itself as a high priority in health policy, we have been provided with a multitude of explanations for the rapid rise in cost of care as well as proposals for holding down these expenditures (Jain, 1983). These explanations ranged from (a) a fee-for-service/cost reimbursement profit-oriented free enterprise system, to (b) exponential growth of technology, to (c) the tyranny of regulations, to (d) separation of payment responsibility from the decision to seek care, to (e) undue emphasis on treatment and prolongation of life, to (f) the weak voice of the consumers, to (g) a conspiracy of providers, to (h) the use of licensing and accreditation to establish monopolistic control, to (i) waste and fraud.

Ongoing medical innovations mandate a constant re-evaluation of the entire health care system. For example, where should priorities be set among the following areas: preventing disease, uncovering more disease by better diagnosis, treating disease and disability, and using new technologies to reorganize care? Or, how much emphasis should be put on additional research for the creation of additional health care technologies?

The history of the health system in the United States provides numerous illustrations that excessive emphasis in any one area tends to create upsets in another area. For example, in order to coordinate the specialists, allied health personnel, and complex diagnostic and therapeutic equipment involved in modern medical practice, the services and facilities must be geographically focused. The ever-increasing narrow, medical specialists' output creates increasing chances for technical errors, fragmented and "depersonalized" care and communications breakdowns. This environment in turn, impacts on the number of malpractice claims and the size of awards to patients. This in turn, results in health providers paying more for professional liability insurance coverage. Health providers react to this situation by furnishing more services than they would otherwise; a practice commonly referred to as "defensive medicine." Defensive medicine, in turn, contributes to increased national health care expenditures (AMA, 1984).

Another example is the major trend in health policy analysis some refer to as the "new reductionism" (Sirott & Waitzkin, 1984). This mid-1970's approach to health care policy was characterized by an expression of genuine skepticism about the value of medical care with all of its technological advances. At this time, a consensus emerged that new breakthroughs in medical research, increased availability of medical services and traditional public health measures would be increasingly unable to produce the dramatic improvements in health that the public had come to expect from them. The disenchantment with the technological world order resulted in the rediscovery of prevention, including the emergence of an emphasis on holism and self-care.

Holism and Self-Care

Although there are many variations on the theme of holism and self-care, these trends have certain characteristics of social movements. In general, holism stands opposed to Western medicine, which claims a scientific, technological base. Therapies vary widely, yet, each sees a person as a whole being, illness as a disruption of personal integration, and therapy as aiming at a healthier reintegration of the total being (Sirott & Waitzkin, 1984).

Self-care involves the attitudes and techniques by which individuals assume responsibility for maintaining health and treating illness, often in a group setting. The individual's ability to prevent illness is made possible through lifestyle changes (1984).

Self-care received the support of business, government and philanthropies in the 1970s (USPHS, 1980). Agencies of the U.S. government have published manuals promoting self-care and prevention and have funded the formation of self-care programs. A number of position papers and government pronouncements have appeared that place the primary responsibility for health on the individual's life-style.

Among the more prominent and thoughtful experts concerned with the relationship between health and society are Victor Fuchs, Ivan Illich, John Knowles, Anne and Herman Sommers and Amitai Etzioni.

Advocating a major revolution in perception, Illich (1974) believes that the institution of modern medicine exerts a pernicious effect on society and should be dismantled. The arguments of *Medical Nemesis* suggest that the basic problem is the emergence of medicine as a strong and coercive institution in industrial society. Because this institution limits the individual's capacity for personal growth and self-care, it should be dismantled. He suggests that medicine has an iatrogenetic effect at three levels--the clinical, social, and structural. He suggested that only a substantial reduction in total medical outputs could foster autonomy in health and in sick care, and thereby make it effective. He advocates the development of the individual's capacity for coping.

In *Who Shall Live?*, Fuch (1976) puts the responsibility for health on factors that are in the individual's sphere of control and not subject to societal intervention. He argues that current variations in health among individuals and groups are largely determined by genetic factors, environment, and life-style. His arguments are based on data from a comparison of death rates in Nevada and Utah. "Mormon" Utah has lower death rates from cirrhosis and cancer. Fuchs argues that it is the hurried lifestyle and use of tobacco and alcohol in Nevada that causes higher death rates there.

According to Fuchs, an economist, the principal problems of the American health care system include limited accessibility to services for some groups, poor overall public health levels compared with other countries, and high costs. The high costs of medical care and the ever increasing health problems tax available resources; creating a scarcity of resources and a need to learn to allocate them as efficiently as possible. In order to do this, it is necessary to find the proper balance between individual (personal) and collective (social) responsibility. While he acknowledges the many inequities of the nineteenth-century's unbridled individualism, he chastises the current denial of individual responsibility for their own distress and the idealization of social responsibility. For Fuchs, the notion that everyone has "the right to health" is misleading, for positive health can be achieved only through intelligent effort on the part of each individual.

John Knowles in his essay, "The Responsibility of the Individual" in *Doing Better and Feeling Worse* (1977), discusses what he sees as the barriers to the assumption of personal responsibility for one's own health. Lack of knowledge, lack of interest, and a culture which has progressively eroded the idea of individual responsibility are the barriers.

Knowles cites the famous Belloc and Breslow study (1973) that showed life expectancy and health are significantly related to several basic health habits including:three meals a day and no snacks, moderate weight and exercise, adequate sleep, no smoking, and only moderate amounts of alcohol. Knowles also emphasizes that historically, control of communicable disease depended as much or more upon broad environmental changes attendant upon improved housing, nutrition, and sanitation, as it did upon individual behavior and knowledge. Knowles states that the individual has the power and the moral responsibility to maintain his own body's health by the observance of simple, prudent rules of behavior relating to sleep, exercise, diet and weight, alcohol and smoking. He further states that these simple rules can be understood and observed by the majority of Americans.

He specifically argues that the white, affluent middle class will follow these rules because they are well-educated. Social policies should first improve education, employment, civil rights, and economic levels, and then improve accessibility to services because fear, ignorance, desperation, and superstition all conspire against even the desire to remain healthy.

Victim Blaming

Obviously these approaches to health and disease prevention did not go without attack. Among those who strongly disagreed with Illich, Fuchs and others were William Ryan (1971), Robert Crawford (1977), and Vicente Navarro (1976).

One of the more profound critiques of individual responsibility for health care, carried to the extreme, comes in the form of victim blaming. Both Ryan and Crawford discuss the reductionism that leads to the conclusion that an individual's sickness or early death is ultimately his own fault. These arguments are really not new to our culture.

Historically, our Puritan ancestors believed "the sins of the fathers are visited upon the sons," and illness was a result of personal sins (Starr, 1982). Subtle "victim blaming" can lead to ideologically legitimating cut-backs in medical services on the basis that it is not society, but the individual, who has the ultimate cure for disease and disability. For example, the fear that AIDS may spread from the homosexual community and other high risk groups to the general heterosexual population has provoked controversy and demands that restrictions be imposed on victims of the disease (Jonsen, Cooke & Koenig, 1986).

Development of Social Medicine

Concurrent with the trends toward increased specialization and emphasis on individual prevention of illness was the emergence of a form of "social medicine." Social medicine promoted prevention, cure and treatment, and rehabilitation by trying to understand the total person in relation to the total social, cultural, and physical environment. On the treatment side, social medicine has concentrated most heavily on prevention rather than cure.

The perspectives of Anne and Herman Sommers (1977), in *Health and Health Care* are in keeping with the concept of social medicine. Sommers and Sommers suggest that health care should be a part of a larger framework of broad policy of "health promotion." If the individual's responsibility is to be effectively discharged, it must be supported by social programs designed to provide the essential environmental protection, health information, and access to health care when needed.

Sommers and Sommers see the policies of individual responsibility and social responsibility as complementary, not antithetical, as Illich claims. They see that neither can be fully effective without the other. Health, to them, is not a commodity that one individual can bestow on another. Health, they say, cannot be legislated nor assured by regulation. For the most part, health has to be earned and maintained by the individual. They also admit that the individual's conditions of life are, in large degree, the product of social and political choices on the part of society.

Amitai Etzioni (1978) argues along these same lines when he suggests that the assumption that society may expect vast improvements in the health of the nation from individual efforts is overly simplistic. It is his opinion that the health and individual responsibility argument may overestimate the health benefits which will occur from personal habit changes, and ignores the impact of societal constraints on individual will.

Etzioni suggests that a health policy that promotes curbing unhealthy habits and encourages healthy ones through societal action is more ethical and feasible than one focusing on health as an individual responsibility.

The federal government acknowledged the importance of health promotion or wellness programs by developing a series of health promotion/disease prevention strategies for achieving further improvements in the nation's health. These strategies called for improvement of the health of Americans at the five major life stages: infancy, childhood, adolescence, adulthood, and old age. Specific and measurable objectives were quantified, and a request was made for a national commitment to reduce the rates of premature death and disability (USPHS, 1980).

William Campbell Felch (1986) has expressed some well founded concerns about the prevention enterprise. He suggests that prevention, in the process of expanding, has picked up some dubious remedies: copper bracelets, megavitamins and trace elements, and the flood of diet books, to name a few.

It is his opinion that the "scientific" literature is full of dogmatic and contradictory opinions which need to acquire scientific grounding or be eliminated. He believes it is time that organized medicine identified preventive measures with sound scientific underpinnings and that it educated practitioners about their judicious application. Society, in turn, needs to develop a healthy skepticism concerning quick cures for major health problems.

PUBLIC INTEREST

This summary of differing philosophies toward the provision of health care emphasizes the potential conflict between freedom of the individual and the requirements of bureaucratic rationalization to ensure that adequate services are available for everyone (Jaques, 1983).

Despite the fact that each approach presents real or potential advantages, each also manifests problems. These radically differing views also underscore the difficulties faced when policy and science interact.

In practical terms, serving the public interest in health planning must include improving health and the prospects for it, as well as providing adequate quality and equitable distribution of service (Milio, 1981). Health promotion efforts currently include identification of persons at risk of disease, such as hypertension and diabetes; educational efforts to change behavior, such as nutrition counseling and smoking cessation programs; stress management; exercise and weight reduction programs; and employer/employee programs to reduce exposure to hazardous substances or unsafe practices in the work place.

The patterns of lifestyle of healthy individuals suggest that each seeks, within the limits of their awareness, what will bring the largest gain in return for cost. The decisions people make which form their patterns of behavior--when they participate in prevention activities, and how they respond to advice given them--are not strictly a matter of free choice. Rather, they are choices made among a limited range of options open to them. To be motivated, the individual must be convinced there is a payoff. Few would argue about payoff with regard to immunizations, but there is less agreement about the benefits of alterations in lifestyle (Rogers, Eaton & Bruhn, 1981). They are likely to make the "easiest" choices, the ones promising the greatest gain for the least cost. The limitations on those opportunities come from both their personal, social and economic circumstances and from the system of health services available to them.

Studies show that both attitudes and knowledge can change the way people view their circumstances. However, whether knowledge and attitudes translate into behavior is quite another matter (Thompson, 1978; Goodstadt, 1986; Fortmann et al., 1981).

This is borne out by the success rate of health education programs in changing peoples' behavior. Various campaigns to change life-style patterns which were general, complex, and integrated into everyday living, and therefore less under individual control, such as weight loss and exercise, were much less successful than those which were fairly specific such as taking hypertensive drugs or smoking cessation (Farquhar et al., 1977).

It has also been demonstrated that new knowledge and attitudes are often not necessary to modify behavior. Readily available access to services, or provision of new opportunities to obtain services at low relative cost, encourage new patterns of behavior. Not only may knowledge or attitudes change quite apart from behavior, but they also may and often do, change after new patterns of behavior have been adapted, bringing them in line with actual experiences (Milio, 1981).

Innovation involves new behavior, new habits, new interlocking expectations which we call roles in social theory, and it even involves new interlocking patterns of roles, which we call institutions or practices. On the individual level, innovation implies some real change in our perceptions and implies a structural change in our commitments to actions.

So long as acute care interventions are dramatic and well publicized (artificial hearts and liver transplants) they capture the imagination and empathy of millions, consequently generating political support for the "miracle" of medicine regardless of cost. The success of a prevention policy in motivating people is limited by the scarcity of scientific evidence of its benefits (Russell, 1984; 1986).

Roemer (1984) contends that a health policy emphasizing prevention is quite sound, and should not be regarded as antagonistic to a national program of medical care for all. Good medical care enhances the opportunities for prevention and is more apt to be less expensive than separate arrangements. Integrated prevention and medical care, if only because of economies of scale and savings on such a common item as transportation makes good sense. Most important is the practical convenience for people, the administrative efficiency, and the greater community impact of providing preventive and treatment services at the same local facilities, often at the same time, that are less expensive than separate arrangements (Yankauer, 1981). This will require a reorientation by physicians as to their role in preventive services, for the average physician sees his role as personal and curative (Freymann, 1975), and unrelated to government sponsored mass collective actions.

In order to encourage the public to "buy into" prevention activities it may be necessary to alter reimbursement policies and change the way individuals perceive physician and health provider roles.

IV

Economic Significance

In most societies, market forces are the principal factor influencing the development and adoption of technologies (Teich, 1981). But in health care, they are at best an imperfect mechanism for ensuring that the development and introduction of new technologies will be socially and environmentally acceptable. Here, market processes can just as easily work to perpetuate the use of inappropriate or unnecessary medical technologies (OTA, 1984).

Development and adoption of medical technology is most often the result of circumstances of the environment (Tanon & Rogers, 1975). These circumstances include financing methods, market conditions, and government programs. A large part of the growth in health care in recent years, has been due to the enormous quantity of resources spent in providing medical care. The rapid development of expensive medical technology while benefiting many patients, has also created rapidly rising health costs.

IMPACT OF TECHNOLOGY ON MEDICAL COSTS

According to the Comptroller General's Report on national health care expenditures, medical technology has been identified as one of the key health care cost containment issues that American society needs to address (1985). These expenditures have been especially troublesome in the Medicare program; an area in which OMAR exercises a great deal of influence.

Recent efforts to access the impact of technology on health care spending have produced mixed results; demonstrating the difficulty in generalizing on the subject (OTA, 1982). Among the factors which

29

complicate the assessment are the (a) changing nature of medical advances, (b) changes in the health status of the population resulting from the increased prevalence of chronic diseases, and (c) differences in specific technology related costs.

One example of cost *savings* involves situations where drug therapy is substituted for hospitalization in the treatment of tuberculosis. Another example of decreased medical costs involve the use of penicillin, sulfa, vaccines and other antibiotics instead of institutionalized medical care (Comptroller General, 1985). On the other hand, certain technologies which have high initial costs and/or operating costs often *increase* medical costs. In addition, technological advances which lower per unit costs (automated clinical laboratories) may decrease or increase overall medical costs, depending on the extent of their application (1985).

The federal government has also increased its emphasis on health promotion or wellness programs designed to increase consumer awareness of potential benefits of practicing healthy lifestyles. Unfortunately, believing that prevention offers savings as well as better health has put many of its proponents at a disadvantage (Russell, 1986). In actual fact, most evaluations of preventive measures show that while such interventions may improve health they usually add to the total medical bill. Because it takes many years to acquire statistics on prevention activities, there is currently insufficient data to conclude that prevention produces non-medical savings most of the time, or that such savings usually outweigh the addition to medical costs.

Louise B. Russell contends this lack of data should not penalize the entire prevention effort. She suggests that if choices need to be made regarding what services and programs should be supported, prevention should not be subjected to a more stringent standard than acute care. The test should always be: Is the gain in health a reasonable return for the resources expended (1986)?

What has become clear however, is that certain medical technologies, e.g., organ transplants, if widely used, increase expenditures because on a per unit basis, they require large quantities of health care resources.[1] On the other hand, the increased use of certain other technologies, e.g., personal computers, could have a significant beneficial impact on the unnecessary use of health services.[2]

Attempts to control the rate of increase of costs and adoption of medical technology at the federal level have largely been regulatory (Banta, Burns & Behney, 1983). These regulations are primarily designed to avoid the introduction of excessively costly or potentially injurious technology. Examples of such undertakings include the health planning program and the Professional Standards Review Organizations program (PSRO), which evaluate the necessity of services rendered by physicians to patients, the appropriateness of the facilities where these services are provided and the quality of service or care provided. While both programs have been judged to have failed in their attempt to control costs (1983), an analysis by Cromwell and Kaanak in 1982, found that rates of technology diffusion in states with mandated rate settings were definitely lower than elsewhere.

At the federal level, the Social Security Amendments of 1983, provided new guidelines with regard to the prospective reimbursement issue. In this legislation, the Congress changed cost based reimbursement to payment of pre-determined amounts (Prospective Payment System [PPS]) for acute care hospitals treating Medicare beneficiaries (Wilensky, 1984). Since the plan was not fully implemented until fiscal year 1987, data does not appear to be available assessing the effect of the PPS on the adoption of medical technology. In fact, OTA's most recent report on the subject (1985) does not evaluate the PPS; instead, it identifies the kind of information necessary to develop an appropriate evaluation of the system over the next five years.

Current federal focus on basic research has produced a deliberate division of labor between the government and private industry (Bartocha & Solomon, 1985). This division of labor as it relates to biomedical basic, applied, and innovation R&D and has also had substantial financial consequences. Clearly it is in the interest of companies to stress the most lucrative areas of science. This has reflected itself in the total dollar expenditures associated with the Medicare Program and the frequent overuse of the technological interventions paid for through our reimbursement policies (OTA, 1984). Market imperfections which include extensive insurance coverage, private and public third-party reimbursement, and the arcane nature of contemporary science itself, further prevent the competitive market from achieving truly efficient outcomes.

According to some experts, one of the ramifications of the split in focus between basic research and commercialization activities has been that costly technological advances have been introduced, diffused, and utilized before their effectiveness was clearly demonstrated (Rosenfeld, 1983). Many individuals are of the strong opinion that this situation could be alleviated if technology was thoroughly evaluated before extensive use and that expensive equipment and/or resources be shared (Comptroller General, 1985). Others fear that such a process would all but stop technological development because of the time each evaluation would take (OTA, 1985). Still others believe that our traditional responses, which allow uncoordinated change to proceed or modify parts of the health system piecemeal through the political process are inadequate to deal with the complexities of our health care system (Thier, 1986).

FEDERAL EFFORTS TO CONTROL COSTS

Controlling costs related to biomedical technology innovation requires attention to what opportunities will be foregone. Unfortunately, we continue to lack fundamental information on what is useful and what is not (Comptroller General, 1985). There is general concern for the nation's lack of an officially stated national technology policy.

In the current Congress, the Committee of Science, Space, and Technology began an extensive study of technology policy to identify problems associated with our ad hoc policy for technology. The approach is to focus on the government's relationship to the private-sector role. Factors such as the environment for innovation and creativity, the level and focus of R&D funding, the improvement of technology transfer, worker retraining, and identification of essential industries and technologies is to be examined. The study also is examining technology transfer comprehensively; looking at research universities, mission agencies, federal laboratories and corporate R&D centers. Major non-technical influences such as government regulation, tax policy, venture capital and industrial management is also to be addressed (Roe, 1987).

It is possible that government does not make a sufficiently large contribution to developing the pre-commercial structure of health care technologies. Rather, it concentrates most of its support on the links in the innovation process related to discovery phases and leaves commercial development to industrial strategies designed to take advantage of federal health care reimbursement policies.

The recent history of the health care system in the United States provides examples of the strategic use of technology by pharmaceutical, medical device and instrumentation manufacturers to gain profitability and market leadership (Banta, Burns & Behney, 1983).

Federal policies and programs such as tax structure, monetary policy, regulation, patent policy and aspects of national health policy also have an important impact on biomedical innovation. While these broad policies may nurture the scientific and medical professions and the economy in general, they seem to fail to provide sufficient conditions for the realization of the potential for prevention innovations.

REIMBURSEMENT POLICIES

Federal "protection" in the form of reimbursement policies, particularly third-party payments for medical care have been shown to profoundly affect the adoption and use of medical technology by providers (OTA, 1985). This observation is supported by a study conducted by Logsdon (1983; 1986). The INSURE project, a clinical model of preventive services developed from epidemiological reports and clinical trials found in the medical literature and from consensus standards, suggests that the inertia about prevention noted within the private practitioner group may be overstated. Physicians will give patients prevention and health promotion information if the materials are systematically organized, and if they are *reimbursable*.

Reimbursement policies which disrupt the free marketplace, offer providers few incentives to with-hold the use of technology or to choose a less costly alternative (Tanon & Rogers, 1975). Where the prevention, rehabilitative and ambulatory market is not large enough to justify the investment required, these same payments may act as disincentives to innovations.

It is in those areas where complementary efforts at "technology pull" through intervention in products and markets that appear to be best associated with successful prevention innovations. Such was the case with pneumococcal vaccine.

In 1979, OTA estimated that if the vaccine were provided through a public program to keep costs down, medical expenditures for people over 45 would be a few dollars less than without the vaccine. Despite the fact that the vaccine ended up adding to the total medical spending, the cost was quite reasonable for the gain of a healthier life by people over 65. Congress voted to cover pneumococcal vaccine under Medicare, not because it was free, but because it brought better health at a reasonable cost (Russell, 1986).

CHAPTER IV NOTES

[1] For example, a 1985 Comptroller General's report states that increased use of technologies such as organ transplants, renal dialysis and respiratory therapy have been part of a revolution in what the system can provide and what the public expects.
[2] A 1985 Office of Technology Assessment report stated that increased use of care-giving technologies designed to allow elderly persons to remain at home longer and the increased use of computers could provide elderly persons with health information on diet, exercise, drug interactions and monitor vital signs that could reduce Medicare costs.

V

The Role of the Investigator

OVERVIEW

A number of studies supported by the NSF in the late 1970s provided valuable insights into the dynamics of the industrial innovation process (Booz-Allen & Hamilton, 1963; Battelle Institute, 1973; Myers & Marquis, 1969; Denver Research Institute, 1976). These studies ran the gamut from determining why the failure rate for industrial technological innovations is so high to identifying root causes of socially counter-productive actions to desirable innovations.

In the attempt to understand the forces which drive the industrial innovation process, eight characteristics were noted to have considerable significance (Schon, 1967). These reported characteristics include:

1. Early recognition of need.
2. Independent inventor.
3. Technical entrepreneur.
4. External innovation.
5. Government financing.
6. Informal transfer of knowledge.
7. Supporting innovations.
8. Unplanned confluence of technology.

Upon examination of the frequency of occurrence of the various characteristics it was noted that recognition of technical opportunity ranked high among the factors: the opportunity to create an improved product being a strong motivating force in the innovation process. The significance of the technical entrepreneur and the recognition of need also ranked high (Myers & Marquis, 1969; Schon, 1967).

Studies also indicated that key individuals tend to be active in the innovation for long periods of time. In the case of innovations such as the development of Organophosphorus Insecticide and the early oral contraceptives, successful inventors and entrepreneurs persisted in spite of numerous problems--which were eventually overcome (Schon, 1967).

While independent inventor and technical entrepreneurial environments may differ from each other, there is usually commonality in the requirement for organizational and financial support. The task of acquiring financing for the small business-based investigator presents a significantly different situation from that faced by the investigator who is associated with a university or some other group.

Often, institutions and groups have greater experience and expertise in locating sources of funds and in following the necessary procedures to obtain them. The larger and richer localities and the more elite institutions have developed considerable "grantsmanship," i.e., management skills and personal contacts that help them obtain R&D funds. This statement is borne out by funding statistics produced by the Grants Finance Branch of NIH, which show that 59 of the 60 largest extramural awards in fiscal year 1986 were made to prestigious universities.[1]

Statistics show that in any one year in this country, up to 600,000 small firms open for business (Wetzel, Jr., 1983). Of those, probably no more than 1100-1200 attract the investment interest of the institutionalized, formal venture capital community. The rest meet their capital needs from their own resources or government support.

Therefore, to all prospective participants, identifying a potential source of funding becomes an important first step in the innovation process. If the goal is to obtain federal backing, the most straightforward means to such source identification is to focus on one's particular industry and the federal agency interested in it. Each of these agencies will on request, make available all information related to their particular requirements for funding.

FUNDING

In order to address the funding needs of the profit-oriented investigator, NIH opened its grants mechanism to private industry in 1982; permitting companies to compete directly with universities and not-for-profit organizations for research dollars. The major difference between profit-oriented competition for grant funding and the traditional contract funding was the disallowance of a fixed fee (profit).

As NIH controls more than two-thirds of the federal expenditures for biomedical R&D (Jacoby, 1983), it offers the best opportunities for the researcher to obtain federal funding. NIH is also a highly competitive marketplace. Recent budget cuts affecting this agency have increased competition for their limited resources. Such competition is exacerbated by previous experience and unpublished statistics that indicate that NIH's legislated peer review process does not enthusiastically support for-profit applications. This may be due to the fact that industry represents direct competition for the universities which rely heavily on NIH support. Data from the Grants Finance Branch indicate that in fiscal year 1986, of the $3,436,097,091 in total awards, $50,741,108 was given to private industry. This amount is less than 2 percent of the total domestic awards for fiscal year 1986. Of the $50,741,108 which made its way into the private sector, $44,571,717 were in the form of Small Business Innovation Program set-asides.[2]

Another funding route open to small business is the University-Industry Research Relationships (UIRR), which the government also has the capacity to supplement (Blumenthal, Gluck, Louis, Stato & Wise, 1986). The University-Industry research relationship, however, is not easily established where product development is involved. In competition for funding, the faculty/student environment of a university gives it the advantage of large amounts of discretionary time available to the faculty and a large body of very low-paid graduate students who serve as apprentices on research projects. This is in contrast to the industrial environment concerned with innovation, which has a multitude of very focused and applied problems searching for new techniques and methods by which they might be solved. That is, there is limited discretionary time, and usually few or no very low-paid employees to work on research projects.

These major differences of institutions and people suggest opportunities for cooperation rather than competition for funds. Unfortunately, the special nature of the reward structures are frequently not compatible. For example, any collaboration that forecloses the possibility of open publication is doomed by the academic personnel to failure. Since commercial success is often based upon secrecy, contract negotiations in this area of cooperation are often unresolvable.

There have also been suggestions that there is a decided lack of interest on the part of many university personnel in converting science and technology into a form that the market place will find useful. Many academics simply eschew involvement in what they consider to be another and an unfriendly world; they consider successful innovators in this other world "different" (Westwood and Brupbacher, 1985). According to Roland Tibbetts of the National Science Foundation (NSF), this tendency may be changing. He states that increasingly, NSF SBIR proposals also include university collaboration, with approximately one-half of all grantees utilizing university scientists and engineers in fiscal year 1987.[3]

Narrowing down the numerous sources of funding to identify the most appropriate vehicle requires both a considerable investigation and a comprehensive understanding of the potential benefits and shortcomings inherent in the various mechanisms. Just as with ideas, sources of business development financing are found in both the private and public sectors. Among the private venture capital private partnerships and corporations, publicly held venture firms, venture capital funds formed by banks and bank holding companies, divisions of major corporations, affiliates of investment banking firms, and direct venture investment activity by insurance companies, pension funds or investment advisory firms (Pratt & Morris, 1984). Several sources of government assisted funding include Small Business Investment Companies (SBIC) and Minority Enterprise Small Business Investment Companies (MESBIC)--which are privately capitalized venture capital firms, licensed and regulated by the Small Business Administration--and the SBA's unique Small Business Innovation Research Program (SBIR).

The small percentage of the total NIH research budget made available to small businesses lends credence to the motivations for the establishment of the SBIR program (P. L. 97-219). That is, despite the significant increases in available funds, the small, technology-based firm continues to receive an insignificant percentage of funding.

The signing of the Small Business Innovation Development Act of 1982 was an attempt to insure that an adequate share of R&D funding from federal agencies was made available to small business. This legislation contains the following purposes:

1. To stimulate technological innovation.
2. To use small business to meet a portion of federal research and development needs.
3. To increase private sector commercialization of innovations derived from federal R&D.
4. To foster and encourage participation by minority and disadvantaged persons in technological innovation.

Administrative oversight of the implementation of the SBIR program by the affected agencies is the responsibility of the Small Business Administration (SBA). Both the Office of Science and Technology Policy and the SBA are required to monitor the SBIR programs, and annually provide House and Senate Small Business Committees with any recommendations they deem appropriate.

The SBIR program, as outlined in the legislation, consists of three phases:

1. Phase I--has as its objective to establish the technical merit and feasibility of proposed research or R&D efforts that may ultimately lead to commercial products, and to determine the quality of performance of the small business awardee or organization. Awards normally may not exceed $50,000, for a period normally not to exceed six months.
2. Phase II--has as its objective the continuation of the research or R&D efforts initiated in Phase I, which are likely to result in commercial products or services. Awards may not exceed $500,000, for a period normally not to exceed two years.
3. Phase III--has as its objective the pursuit of commercialization of the product by the small business with non-governmental funds.

The initial passage of the SBIR Program was not without formidable opposition. Critics of the legislation voiced serious concern about its influence on biomedical research.[4] These individuals argued that the NIH, by setting aside a particular dollar amount that must be awarded or lost, would compromise the peer review process at the NIH if it encouraged funding of less than the most meritorious applications. They also thought that the national biomedical research effort would be damaged by further reducing research funding allocations to universities and research institutions. The Federation of American Societies for Experimental Biology, for one, has gone on record as being concerned that SBIR is being made permanent "without having been evaluated for its effectiveness in achieving its statutory objectives and for its efficiency in the use of federal research dollars" (NCI's SBIR awards, 1986, pg. 3).

This concern for the quality of the SBIR applications apparently is not shared by the NIH. The NCI Deputy Director told a House Small Business Subcommittee that response to the Fiscal Year 1986 SBIR program announcement was more than adequate to allow for the selection of high quality grant and contract awards. He noted that approximately 2,180 organizations had submitted SBIR proposals, and a total of 570 had been awarded to account for the entire $11.35 million set aside (1986).

COMMERCIALIZATION OF FEDERALLY SUPPORTED RESEARCH

Almost as important as funding is the issue of commercialization rights. Patent programs should be reviewed to determine whether the agency supports a program which fosters commercialization of federally funded inventions.

The Stevenson-Wydler Technology Innovation Act of 1980 (P. L. 96-480), was designed to foster commercialization of federally funded inventions. In order to comply with this legislation, the NIH established a NIH/DHHS Patent Program. It is designed to stimulate the growth in availability and widespread applications of safe and efficacious health care technology innovations through their commercialization by the private sector. Under this program, the NIH receives invention reports filed by NIH employees, grantees and contractors for evaluation to determine whether the invention should be patented, not patented but made public through publication, or neither.

In contrast to the NIH/DHHS program, the SBIR programs offer the small technology-based firm unprecedented incentives to compete by permitting small firms to retain rights in inventions and technical data derived from the funded work. Except in narrowly defined circumstances, the funding agency will retain only a royalty-free license to use the invention for internal governmental purposes (P. L. 97-219, 1982).

FORCES INFLUENCING INNOVATIONS

This review of the biomedical innovation process suggests that both the federal government and the private sector are important in determining what happens on the biomedical scientific and technological front in the United States. The free enterprise system, while producing a wide variety of products and/or services, has as its primary objective a favorable return on its investment and a special niche in the marketplace. Government, on the other hand, does not define its technical operations by net earnings. Its roles in health care technology are pluralistic in nature, and involve an array of complicated interactions, including basic research, technology assessment and diffusion, and reimbursement for medical care.

Few would argue that the government is the proper and natural source for funding basic biomedical research. Unfortunately, if accomplished in isolation, there is no guarantee that the science being supported will result in technological innovations benefiting society or the economy.

A. J. Gellman points out that scientists should be interested in more than the front end of the innovation process (1985). In fact, he states there is ample evidence to support the hypothesis that innovation processes are carried out more efficiently, and with greater speed, where those who provide underlying science outputs have at least a general understanding of what must happen to these outputs if a useful product or service is to result. He also makes the point that there is no single general case that can be studied to gain a full and relevant understanding of the way conversions of science-to-technology-to-innovations works in every setting. To Gellman, the most efficient means of acquiring knowledge of the innovation process is to identify those forces that impinge upon the different scenes in their own environments.

John Diebold suggests that the goal of a national research strategy should be to unleash the creative energies through incentives and disincentives that ensure the maximum rewards for new scientific discoveries (Shapiro, Diebold, Gorton & Massey, 1986). Diebold supports Gellman's position and underscores the need to understand the mechanisms that carry scientific discoveries from the laboratory to the market place. It is his opinion that the peer review process, which tends to favor "safe" or proven topics of research rather than explore radically new frontiers, exacerbates the problem of delays in bringing scientific discoveries to the marketplace. Despite its obvious merits, peer review seems as sure a roadblock to innovation as the "don't rock the boat" philosophy encountered in bureaucracies.

The assumption is sometimes made that the number of innovations emerging successfully through the innovation process can be increased by increasing the number that begin. This approach requires that more be done to stimulate creativity, to encourage inventions and to increase research and development. The correctness of such a policy has long been an article of faith among many in the R&D field. Put more money into research and development, and there will be more successful industrial innovations. Therefore, providing a highly productive segment of business with greater access to funding would logically lead to a greater number of successful technological innovations. An alternative approach is to attack the barriers to innovation, to find out why innovations fail and make appropriate changes so they are not necessarily blocked. In order to do this, it is necessary to examine actual technological innovations and attempt to determine why they succeeded or failed, with a view to suggesting public policies that might decrease the rate of failure.

The SBIR program has been designed to afford the small business-based investigator a number of unique incentives to participate in the biomedical innovation process (P. L. 97-219). It does this by providing this highly productive segment of business with greater access to funding. What is not known, is whether the funding incentive is enough to drive the innovation process forward. In order to address this question, several different technological innovation products will be examined to identify those forces that either drive the process forward or act as disincentives to continued participation.

CHAPTER V NOTES

[1] Data supplied by the Research and Evaluation Branch (RAEB), Grants Finance Branch, National Institutes of Health.
[2] Data supplied by the RAEB, Grants Finance Branch, National Institutes of Health.
[3] Information supplied by Roland Tibbets, National Science Foundation.
[4] John F. Sherman's testimony presented to the Science, Research and Technology sub-committee at a hearing on passage of HR 4260 and reauthorization of SBIR. July 16, 1986.

VI

Investigative Procedures

STUDY DESIGN

A review of the literature suggests there is limited information describing the nature and effectiveness of federal incentives to commercialize biomedical innovations. To provide an information base from which to formulate beginning statements concerning such factors or actions, eight efforts to obtain federal funding for five different biomedical technology innovations were examined.

First, the various sources of federal funding available to the private sector for the development of biomedical innovations and of the competitive process at NIH were reviewed. The latter included how NIH goes about establishing peer review groups and providing them with training and guidelines. The next attempted action was an analysis of peer review generated *Summary Report of Technical Review* documents for each of the eight innovation proposals. The final step involved the effort to obtain Phase II funding after successfully completing three Phase I efforts.

An exploratory research design (Blalock & Blalock, Jr., 1982) was used for the study. This design was chosen because it permitted characterization of federal incentives and disincentives to participate in the biomedical technology innovation process from several perspectives: the government sponsor, the individual developer and the corporation of which the investigator was a Vice-President. The investigator's attempts to gain federal support to develop "commercializable" biomedical innovations provided the means to identify specific variables affecting the biomedical innovation process at NIH.

The biomedical technology innovation process is described as consisting of eight steps: basic research; applied research; evaluation; assessment of potential value; feasibility for widespread use; education; diffusion; and finally, broad application (USPHS, 1984). Because biomedical technology innovation is a multi-phased process in which each step builds upon the proceeding one, it was necessary to collect a variety of data along a continuum to construct a comprehensive and meaningful list of incentives and disincentives. Data was collected through: (a) an analysis of the various opportunities afforded the small business entrepreneur to enter the innovation process; (b) the conduct of three Phase I projects resulting from successful competition in the SBIR program; (c) an explicit attempt to understand the innovation experience in terms of meanings held by those in the biomedical setting, and (d) an interpretation of the events which took place in the effort to gain financial support for biomedical technology innovation in sufficient detail to provide the reader an understanding of the process.

The premise underlying the decision to use cases from one firm was that it represented a unique opportunity to evaluate multiple, proposed innovations that had passed initial screenings. That is, these proposals were determined to have technical merit by both a peer review group and corporate management. As the investigator was involved in all eight proposals, her daily recording of events and activities provide a continuum of observations. In addition, information contained in peer review *Summary Report of Technical Review* documents is privileged information. As such, it is not available for review by anyone except the investigator's staff, government personnel and peer reviewers.

POTENTIAL FOR BIAS

It is recognized that this investigation may have biases, for the very nature of the exploratory design demands that the investigator become thoroughly immersed in the data and rely very heavily on insight and intuition. There is also the issue of selection bias in data generated by any process other than an experiment with random assignment of subjects to treatments (Campbell, 1979).

An attempt was made to keep objective and subjective observations in proper perspective through the maintenance of a project notebook for each of the three Phase I activities. Details of significant events and activities were recorded on a daily basis. At the end of the study, these observations were grouped according to whether the event or activity as an incentive or a disincentive was perceived.

A conscientious effort was made to provide uniform ratings to the *Summary Report of Technical Review* documents through the use of standardized definitions and interpretations. Where no standard definitions existed, definitions were derived from the literature. These definitions are listed in the Glossary of Terms.

The data in the project notebooks also served as source materials for the preparation of the mandatory Phase I Final Report. Copies of these reports were submitted to the NCI Program Office and the Contracts Office. Evaluation of these reports by both groups resulted in an invitation to submit Phase II proposals. Despite the fact these data were collected at only one firm by one investigator, they represent a comparison of eight separate attempts to obtain funding at three different points in time. All eight proposals were determined to have technical merit through a highly competitive process. A vote for approval means that between six and twelve scientists considered each of the projects to be of sufficient merit to be worthy of support.

This situation also afforded an opportunity to see if similar incentives and disincentives were noted for both successful and blocked innovations. By using only approved projects the possible bias of simultaneous analysis of approved and disapproved projects also was avoided.

A United States Government Accounting Office (USGAO) survey of SBIR funded small businesses conducted during the same period in which this study was being conducted confirmed many of the findings reported here (1987, July). This study goes one step farther in that it deals with factors and actions experienced when approval is given to projects but money is not forthcoming. In this respect, this research may be less biased than the USGAO survey which interviewed only those firms conducting funded research.

DEFINITIONS AND CATEGORIZATION

Data gathered in this case study fall into two categories. The first category contains procedures and problems likely to be encountered by all would-be participants in the biomedical innovation process. The second category includes participant observations directly related to the researcher's experiences.

To simplify the comparison and analysis of the data, a classification system was developed by first defining incentives and disincentives and then cataloging them as Primary or Secondary. Primary Incentives or Primary Disincentives categories describe those situations or events that appear in contractual or other formal documents. They describe factors or events that are likely to be encountered by all would-be participants in the biomedical innovation process who are interested in commercializing a particular innovation.

The Secondary Incentives and the Secondary Disincentives categories include specific actions and conditions which either helped or hampered attempts to commercialize the biomedical innovation. These actions were not specifically intended to affect the end product. Subcategories of both Primary and Secondary groupings identify whether incentives and disincentives held social or economic implications for either the investigator or the investigator's firm. Disincentives were sub-classified according to categories defined for the actors in the innovation process: the government and the developer.

SOURCES OF DATA

The biomedical technology innovation process at NIH operates in a multidimensional, complex, and frequently uncertain environment. For the purposes of this study, environment consists of factors which not only are outside of the company's control but which influence, in part, how the corporation performs. Things within the control of the company are resources or means that the company may use in whatever way it finds appropriate. Data gathered in this project represent exchanges between the NIH biomedical environment and the investigator's company.

Sources of information in this project were discussions with NIH administrators involved in the SBIR process, contract correspondence, government publications describing program objectives, and technical review reports derived from peer review group evaluations of the proposals. The flow relationship of information between the NIH biomedical environment and the investigator's firm is depicted in Figure 1. The box labeled "Biomedical Environment" represents the various components of the environment from which information was obtained or information was sought. The box labeled "Corporation" lists the sources of internal information available within the company. Upper management, of which the investigator was a part, relies primarily on information external to the organization for decision making purposes.

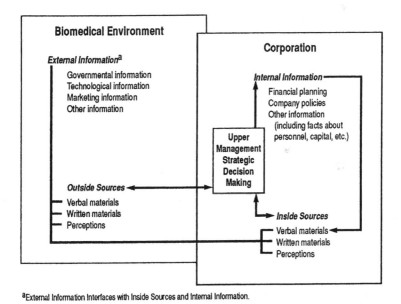

[a]External Information Interfaces with Inside Sources and Internal Information.

Figure 1. Flow relationship of information between the biomedical environment and the corporation.

The discussions held with administrators responsible for the SBIR program at NIH and the NCI elicited information describing administrative procedures used in both the SBIR grant and contract application and review processes. Topics covered included application procedures, procedures for forming peer review committees, and guidelines provided to individual reviewers. As there is never enough funding to support all approved projects, the researcher was also interested in how the institutes decided which of the many approved projects would receive funding. The conversations with SBIR Administrators were not conducted as formal interviews but rather as requests for information. This approach was used to evaluate these discussions from the perspective of the investigator trying to obtain assistance in applying for NIH R&D funding.

Summary Report of Technical Review documents for seven of the eight proposals were obtained through written requests to NIH officials responsible for the specific topic areas. These served as a source of data for identifying Secondary Incentives and Developer Disincentives.

DATA GATHERING

Four major activities provided the data gathered for this study. The first one involved deciding whether to use the Request for Proposals (RFP), the Request for Applications (RFA), the basic grant (R01), or the Small Business Innovation Research (SBIR) award funding mechanism. Once the choice was made, the next steps involved the preparation and submission of contract and grant applications. The final activity centered around the implementation and analysis of the three funded Phase I projects. Details involved in each of these activities are presented below.

Choosing the Funding Mechanism

An assessment of available funding mechanisms was made to determine which to include in this study. This was done through environmental scanning, a process which consisted of general information gathering, monitoring trends, investigating opportunities, and acquiring application forms and guidelines for research proposals (Shoderbek, Shoderbek & Kefalas, 1980).

General Information Gathering. Information regarding happenings in the biomedical research field was reviewed daily. News media, data gathered from government publications and visits to government agencies provided information concerning shifting trends, new opportunities for support in field of interest and federal funding activity.

Scanning. Scanning consisted of gathering information on what was being done in the health promotion/disease prevention area. This type of review provided a current awareness of business opportunities across all agencies of the federal government. In this mode, information was obtained through professional and society journals, specialized journals such as the *Commerce Business Daily, Science,* and the *Cancer Letter,* to name a few. These general information sources of support serve one purpose: to identify which sectors offer business opportunities.

Exploration. Exploration refers to the structured effort to search out information identifying the best opportunities available for health related R&D. Traditional federal funding mechanisms such as Request for Proposals (RFP), Request for Applications (RFA), and any specialized funding routes available through the USPHS were investigated. University-industry research relationships, foundations, the venture capital industry, and special interest groups within the government such as the Small Business Administration (SBA) were also reviewed.

Information was obtained from the Division of Research Grants, NIH, with regard to distribution of awards by performers and type of award for Fiscal Years 1981 through 1986.

Research. Research refers to the steps involved in the preparation and analysis of the eight proposals submitted to NCI's SBIR program for Phase I and Phase II funding.

Figure 2 summarizes the process used to build the researcher's biomedical R&D funding information base. Through scanning, the required information necessary to select the most appropriate course of action from those available was possible.

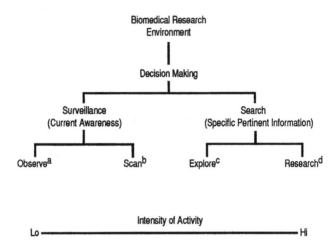

aGeneral information relative to the biomedical reserach field gathered daily from news media, government agency publications and personnel.

bMonitoring of the environment for information concerning health promotion business opportunities through the use of professional and specialized journals.

cInditification of opportunities to acquire funding for helath related R&D.

dMechanism for choosing and submitting proposals.

Figure 2. Summary of the process used to build a biomedical R&D funding information base. Base includes specification of the alternatives possible, consequences of choices, and probabilistic data on the relationship between alternatives and outcomes.

Preparation of Contract and Grant Applications

Selection of Research Topic. Appropriate forms and instructions were obtained for use in applying for NIH traditional and USPHS SBIR Phase I awards. In the case of the SBIR program, this involved obtaining copies of both the current DHHS contract and grant *Omnibus Solicitation* (1985). These documents supply all information necessary to respond to the solicitations, including information on Research Topics which were directly related to agency missions and a description of NIH dual peer review system used to evaluate each application.

Two categories in a list of over fifty from the NCI's portion of the USPHS contract solicitation were targeted for proposal preparation for the first wave. For the second wave, one NCI contract Topic and one NCI grant Topic were selected. In a third wave, Phase II proposals were submitted at the invitation of the NCI, following my successful completion of Phase I efforts. The Topics selected from the solicitations are listed below:

Topic Number 41. *Development of User-Friendly Software for Implementation of the Personal Computer.*

Topic Number 48. *Development of Nutrition Education Materials, Including Computer Software Which Will Result in Long-Term Adherence to Diets Thought to Reduce Cancer Risk.*

Topic Number 38. *Dietary Assessment Systems.*

Topic Number 17B. *Distributed Network for Managing Clinical Trials Data.*

These topics were selected because they represented an area of research in which the investigator's expertise is recognized within the science community. As a result of personal efforts the investigator's firm also is recognized as a leader in state-of-the-art nutrition intervention cancer clinical trials support. This peer recognition was thought to be critical in the NIH competitive environment.

PROPOSAL SUBMISSION

Four Phase I contract applications and one Phase I grant application and three Phase II proposals were prepared and submitted to NCI in three waves. Three Phase I Submissions were completed during the first wave. One Phase I contract and one grant submission were completed during the second wave. In a third wave, three Phase II applications were submitted by invitation from NCI.

These eight proposals represented a total of five "innovations." Three of the four contract proposals involved the development of nutrition education materials which would assist individuals to obtain long-term adherence to diets thought to reduce cancer risk. Specifically these projects were: Estimate-it Calculator; NutriTouch; and Dietary Assessment System. The fourth proposal was to develop epidemiological and statistical programs for the epidemiologist with a personal computer. The grant proposal was to develop a data entry system for clinical trial data incorporating a distributed network. This software system would permit the electronic transfer of patient data from a research facility computer center directly to the NIH computer facility.

PEER REVIEW

All proposals received by NIH were reviewed by a peer review group; also referred to as a study section. A scientist administrator is responsible for the overall coordination and management of the proposal review process (including SBIRs), from the selection of review group members and go through the preparation of the *Summary Report of Technical Review* documents.

At NIH, a distinction is made between administration of grants and of contracts. Many of the administrative procedures, however, are common to both mechanisms. For example, the executive secretary of a Review Group is responsible for providing information necessary to complete a summary statement for an application. The statement reflects the committee's technical evaluation of a particular application. It includes: (a) a factual description of the project; (b) an assessment of the strengths and weaknesses of the application; (c) a recommendation for advisory council approval or disapproval;[1] and (d) a priority score rating that reflects the review group's opinion of the quality of the application recommended for approval.[2]

Summary Report of Technical Review Documents. The format of the technical review reports provides for comments as they relate to: (a) technical approach; (b) personnel; (c) innovation and potential commercial innovation; and (d) facilities and research environment and in the case of Phase II applications (e) progress made in Phase I.

Only approved grant applications receive a priority score. To be approved, an application must be of sufficient merit to be worthy of support based on the appropriate review criteria. These criteria are listed in the orientation materials (See Appendix A). Contract proposals receive technical scores. These scores are also used to determine rank order for funding purposes.

A vote for approval is equivalent to a recommendation that a grant or contract be awarded, provided sufficient funds are available. A priority score rating is also required for grant applications. Each member of the review group records a numerical rating for each approved application. That score is a reflection of the reviewer's private opinion of the merit of the application (USPHS, 1978)

After the scientific merit review, the critiques and applications of the approved research projects are reviewed a second time by the advisory boards of the institutes to which the applications are assigned. This review is to provide an assessment of the project's scientific merit and relevance to the mission and programs.

Following evaluation of grant applications by the review groups, summary documents (with priority scores and names and affiliations of reviewers) are automatically sent to the investigator's organization. Copies of summary documents for successful contract applications must be requested. Information contained in the summary reports is considered highly confidential and copies are not distributed to anyone except the principal investigator's organization.

Grant applications that are approved but not funded may be revised for resubmission at a future receipt date. Contract proposals cannot be resubmitted.

In the review cycle following the proposal submissions, the NCI awarded this investigator's company three of the four contracts. These were to develop the Estimate-it Calculator, NutriTouch and User-friendly Software.

IMPLEMENTING THREE FUNDED PHASE I PROJECTS

As soon as the contracts were negotiated activities were directed toward establishing the technical merit and feasibility of each research project. To keep track of these activities the investigator kept a research notebook for each of the innovations. Details of significant events and activities were carefully documented for use in the mandatory federal contract final report.

Once the projects were completed, the final reports were prepared and submitted to the government. Shortly thereafter, an invitation was received to submit Phase II SBIR proposals for each of the three projects. These also were prepared and submitted. The final event of the data collection process for this dissertation occurred when the *Summary Technical Review* statements for the three Phase II proposals were received. These arrived eleven months after the proposals were submitted.

Appendix B contains a detailed account of one of these projects (Estimate-it) including product evaluation information. The feasibility data and research experience from this project was used to characterize factors affecting the innovation process after the technical feasibility had been proven.

Analysis of the Innovation Process

Classification System. A classification system was developed to characterize factors or actions which encourage or discourage an entrepreneur from participating in the innovation process. This system enabled an evaluation and comparison of data from the four different activities described previously. The events and actions recorded in each of the project notebooks were considered incentives if they facilitated eventual commercialization of the end products. If the incentive appeared in contractual or other formal documents it was classified as a Primary Incentive. If the incentive was not specifically intended to affect a particular innovation, it was considered a Secondary Incentive. Depending upon the context in which they were met, incentives could appear in both categories.

Disincentives were subjected to a modified classification format because they are not as keyed to decision maker levels as are incentives. Innovation is most apt to be impeded or stopped by barriers which affect the actors in innovation stages. Therefore, two broad categories were defined for the actors in the innovation process. The term "sponsor" refers to any government agency actively supporting the innovation process. "Developer" refers to the performer of the R&D. A developer could either be the technical entrepreneur or the corporation.

As the social and economic implications of the Secondary Incentives and Disincentives are not directed toward the endproduct, the chosen method was to examine them in the context of the investigative entrepreneur interacting with the innovation process. To do this, the investigator documented personal experiences and made judgments as to whether the event or activity was perceived as an incentive or as a disincentive.

Because the peer review system at NIH is a key element in the funding process, it too was targeted for observation. These observations included NIH's process for selecting and training peer reviewers and an in-depth analysis of the *Summary Report of Technical Review* documents for each of the innovations.

An attempt was also made to classify comments appearing in each of the *Summary Report of Technical Review* reports for both approved and funded and approved but not funded projects to see if there were any discernible differences. The categories were defined as (a) confusing to interpret, (b) showed lack of understanding of program objectives or (c) were reasonable and appropriate.

Since all eight approved proposals, covering five innovations, were critiqued for this study by the investigator, a special effort was made to standardize definitions and interpretation to provide uniformity of the ratings. Where possible, NIH definitions were used for critical terms. When these were not available, definitions were derived from the literature. These terms are defined in the Glossary of Terms.

CHAPTER VI NOTES

[1]   Approval: The application is of sufficient merit to be worthy of support based on the appropriate review criteria. A vote for approval is equivalent to a recommendation that a grant be awarded provided sufficient funds are available. A priority score rating is required. Disapproval: The application is not of sufficient merit to be worthy of support. Disapproval may also be recommended when hazardous or be recommended as in the case of a supplement deemed to unethical procedures are involved or when no funds can be recommended, as in the case of a supplement deemed to be unnecessary. No priority score rating is required.

[2]   Priority Score Rating: For each application that has been recommended for approval, each member of the study section (review group) records a numerical rating that reflects a private opinion of the merit of the application. The numerical ratings range from 1.0 (the most meritorious) to 5.0 (the least meritorious) with increments of 0.1.

VII

Results and Discussion

The classification system developed for this study provides a means to evaluate federal incentives and disincentives to participate in the biomedical innovation process at two levels. The first describes those actions and events likely to be encountered by most would-be participants in the biomedical innovation process. The second level identifies those actions and conditions which indirectly facilitated or hampered participation in the innovation process. These are described in detail below.

PRIMARY INCENTIVES

Using the NIH Division of Research Grants (DRG) historical financial data presented in Table 1, it was determined that the SBIR program offered the company the strongest alternative to obtain funds for biomedical technology R&D. The DRG funding data revealed only token awards were made to private/for profit organizations before 1983. Because the increases in private sector awards noted from 1983 through 1986 were directly related to the phasing in of SBIR legislation and the fact that the company qualified as a small business, the SBIR was chosen.

Table 2 identifies the Primary Incentives noted in the review of the SBIR as a potential funding source. Incentives include partial, or sometimes, total funding for one or more steps of the innovation process up to the point of commercialization, a set-aside program specifically designed to advance the innovation process, and strong program support from the Small Business Administration. These Primary incentives are discussed in detail below.

Table 1

Domestic Awards Made by NIH for Fiscal Years 1981 Through 1986 by Performer[a]

Fiscal Year	Number	Dollars	Number	Dollars
	Public		Private/Non Profit	
1981	9,177	931,932,554	8,909	1,213,773,408
1982	8,850	957,636,218	8,712	1,258,918,449
1983	9,133	1,059,221,876	9,151	1,419,964,622
1984	9,383	1,213,767,270	9,464	1,610,227,379
1985	9,985	1,411,190,543	9,932	1,840,391,104
1986	10,212	1,469,701,234	10,090	1,915,654,749
	Profit/Large & Unknown		Profit/Small	
1981	0	0	3	40,512
1982	2	210,436	8	531,728
1983	12	1,045,415	139	7,776,509
1984	17	1,970,402	271	23,942,617
1985	16	1,936,673	373	36,722,911
1986	12	1,209,336	478	49,531,772

[a] Data provided by NIH, DRG.

Table 2

Primary Incentives that were Noted in the Review of the SBIR Program as a Potential Funding Source for this Case-Study

---

Generous funding for R&D--Sponsoring agency partially funds the entire innovation process or fully funds one or more steps.

Contracting policy--Sponsoring agency decides on a solicitation strategy to enhance private sector response.

Patent, copyright, and rights-in-data policy--Sponsoring agency makes agreement with developer regarding disposition of proprietary claims over the patent.

Lobbying and testimonies--Efforts by sponsoring agency personnel to influence budgetary or legislative processes.

Continuous Funding Cycle--Application cycle offers multiple opportunities to submit applications each Fiscal Year.

Generous Funding for R&D

Under the phase-in SBIR legislation, all participating agencies, including NIH, were obligated to set-aside one and one-half percent of their R&D budgets by 1986, for small firms to develop commercial applications of federally funded research. This represents a small percentage of the total NIH biomedical research budget. Even so, these funds go a long way toward providing funding for R&D work by many small, innovative science and technology-based companies (USGAO, 1987). This program offered a means to acquire total support for at least two phases of multiple R&D activities. This was considered to be quite generous.

Contracting Policy

In the case of the SBIR program, the contracting policy is dictated by P. L. 97-219, the Small Business Innovation Development Act (SBDA). NIH determines the solicitation strategy through the development of their *Omnibus Solicitation* publications for both grants and contracts. These contain numerous areas of research interest to the government and reflect current agency planning. The set-aside legislation guarantees that at least one and one-half percent of the agency's total research budget will go to small businesses pursuing projects of interest to the federal government.

Patents, Copyrights, and Rights in Data

Small firms are able to retain rights in inventions and technical data derived from the funded work. As was discussed in Chapter V, the SBIR program differs from the NIH/DHHS Patent Program established by NIH in 1980.

Under the NIH/DHHS program, NIH receives invention reports filed by employees, grantees and contractors. These reports are evaluated to determine whether the invention should be patented, not patented but made public through publication, or neither.

In the case of SBIR programs, the funding agency normally will retain only a royalty-free license to use the invention for internal governmental purposes. This policy presents a small business with unprecedented opportunities to retain patent rights as well as rights in data. The latter also includes software developed under the terms of the SBIR funding agreement.

Because the government requires that a plan for raising capital to complete Phase III be included in the Phase II proposal, the firm is forced to look beyond the "front end" of the innovation process. This requirement helps to insure a successful commercialization effort at the conclusion of Phase II.

It was this author's experience that NIH makes a genuine effort to assist potential applicants in the preparation of proposals for SBIR awards. Information packets contained copies of articles describing reasons for poor ratings or disapproval of applications. Also included was information describing the program and the names of individuals to whom questions may be addressed (Cuca, 1983; Vener, 1985). Program Administrators at NIH were also available to answer questions or to refer applicants to the appropriate organization.

Lobbying and Testimonies

The testimonies of SBA officials and the lobbying efforts of The Innovation Development Institute (an organization made up of many small firms participating in the SBIR program) helped to convince Congress it should reauthorize the SBDA of 1982. The reauthorization made the SBIR program permanent; ensuring that one and one-half percent of a participating agency's total R&D funding will continue to be available to small science and technology-based firms.

Continuous Funding Cycle at NIH

The DHHS SBIR program differs from other participating agencies in that its program is administered on a continuing cycle with due dates in April, August and December.[1] Awards are made throughout the year. This presents an advantage for applicants, as they have several opportunities each year to submit proposals. The DHHS program further differs from other agencies in that it supports both a grant and a contract mechanism--offering the firm a choice.

Table 3, NIH Fiscal Year 1986 Awards by Activity, indicates that NIH awarded 316 contracts and 129 grants through the SBIR Program in Fiscal Year 1986, for a total dollar figure of $44,571,717. This represents 90 percent of all the funding awarded to for-profit organizations that year. These figures support my reasoning that the SBIR program offers many incentives to small businesses to compete for biomedical R&D funding.

Table 3
NIH Fiscal Year 1986 SBIR Awards by Activity[a]

Activity	No. of Awards	Dollars Awarded	Average Award
Contracts	316	15,438,355	48,856
Grants	129	29,133,362	225,840
Grand total	445	44,571,717	

[a] Data provided by NIH, DRG.

PRIMARY DISINCENTIVES

Primary disincentives to the use of the SBIR program are presented in Table 4. The list of disincentives has been divided into those that relate to the sponsor (NIH) and those that relate to the developer. For both the sponsor and the developer, funding uncertainly was determined to be a strong disincentive or barrier to biomedical technological innovation.

Lobbying and Testimony

For the sponsor, lobbying against the SBIR program by basic researchers involved in biomedical research serves to stall innovations. This was especially true during Fiscal Year 1986, when efforts were. being made to prevent the reauthorization of the SBDA.

SBIR supporters were quick to note that testimonies by biomedical researcher and physicians in research frequently reflected confusion between business development and product development (Innovation Development Institute, 1986, August). SBIR opponents often argued that the increased availability of venture capital was adequate to meet the needs of small business entrepreneurs. Although venture capital is available to the small business with a good commercial product or service, small businesses must do feasibility testing before venture

Table 4

Primary Disincentives Noted in the Review of the SBIR Mechanism as a Potential Funding Source for this Case-Study

Disincentives for the Sponsor

Lobbying and testimonies - Efforts on the part of lobbies to stall innovations (FASEB).

Low appropriations - Unavailability of funds to adequately support the innovation development.

Lack of administrative support - Lack of support from the Executive Office of the President.

Disincentives for the Developer

Lack of external and/or internal funds - Sponsoring funds are cut off or reduced and/or there is a lack of funds within the firm to carry out the innovation.

Lack of information - Lack of crucial decision-making information with regard to differences between grant and contract submissions.

capital organizations take notice. The SBIR program fills a need by providing money to the small business to complete feasibility testing.

Strong opposition was also expressed by the Federation of American Societies for Experimental Biology (FASEB), an organization which represents scientists involved in basic research efforts. A spokesperson for FASEB indicated concern that SBIR was about to be made permanent "without having been evaluated for its effectiveness in achieving its statutory objectives and for its efficiency in the use of federal research dollars" (NCI's SBIR awards, 1986, p.3). This opinion was not shared by agency SBIR Administrators within NIH and NSF.

Federal administrators indicated that responses to their 1986 program announcements were more than adequate for the selection of high quality grant and contract awards. The program is described as one of the most competitive R&D programs in government. The odds for aspiring SBIR awardees average 21 percent compared to a four-year low of 35.8 percent in 1986, for other funding mechanisms (1986).

Certainly the anti-SBIR lobbying at hearings before the House Oversight Subcommittee served as a potential barrier to the continuation of SBDA. These same opponents, sitting on peer review evaluations of SBIR projects, serve as a major Secondary disincentive to the Developer.

Low Appropriations

Broad, sweeping budget cuts also serve to slow the innovation process by reducing the total number of approved projects supported during any one fiscal year. The NCI itself, suffering from budget cutting measures resulting from the so-called Gramm-Rudman amendment to eliminate the federal budget deficit by 1991, and the federal policy response to the drug problem and the AIDS epidemic, was able to fund only about one third of its Phase II proposals. The budget cuts necessitated the establishment of paylines too high for many approved projects.

Lack of Administrative Support

Within the Executive Office of the President, lack of administrative support for SBIR took the form of administration attempts to reorganize SBA and place its activities within the Department of Commerce.

Lack of Funds

Among the Primary disincentives identified for the Developer were lack of funds, both external and internal, and potential lack of specifics about the program alternatives.

The Developer is affected by those forces and actions which act upon the sponsor. For example, a budget cut was made during the review of the Phase II projects. The result was that approval was received to proceed with eight projects, but money for only three was forthcoming. The company did not have the capital available to take on these projects without federal support.

Lack of Information

A second disincentive for the Developer involved a lack of understanding concerning the differences between SBIR grant and contract applications. The grant mechanism is not often used by private industry because the government does not permit profit or fee to be requested through grants.[2] The grant, which has only been available to profit-oriented organizations since 1982, has not been a particularly lucrative mechanism for private industry.

As noted in Table 3, the number of SBIR grants awarded in Fiscal Year 1986 was smaller than the number of contracts. While the number was smaller, the average dollar amounts were substantially higher than the average award per contract. Since the maximum award for both grant and contract Phase I projects is $50,000, it appears that Phase II awards were also made. The $49,000 average award for contracts further suggests that few Phase II contract awards were made that year. This may be because the review cycle for contracts was reduced from three to one submission date per year.

These data support the notion that the failure to take note of the subtle differences between the grant and contract mechanisms for the majority of the proposals was a barrier to obtaining funding for Phase II projects. While the agency makes clear distinctions between the grant and contract mechanisms through the publication of two separate solicitations, there are minimal differences between the two in terms of preparing applications. In fact, the standard definition for a contract does not fit the SBIR. Rather, the contract more closely resembles the traditional RFA, as it is a request for financial assistance to carry out activities of general interest to the government. The contract, on the other hand, obligates the organization to provide specific end products or services.[3] In reality, the real distinction between the two mechanisms is the addition of fee to the contract.

The similarities in the preparation of the technical approach appears to provide difficulties for peer reviewers as well. The analysis of the peer reviewers comments suggests that both are evaluated in the same way, using the same criteria. If the differences are really so small, it seems inefficient to convene and reimburse two review groups when one would do.

There is, in addition, a significant procedural difference between the grant and the contract mechanisms. This difference involves the ability of grantee applicants to revise and resubmit their applications if they are not funded. According to the NCI Contracting Office, the SBIR contract mechanism follows the guidelines for regular contracts. These guidelines do not allow for resubmission. This investigator was not aware of this difference until after the notification that, although the applications were approved, funding would not be forthcoming. The Contracting Officer responsible for the contract applications suggested she did not know why resubmission was not possible.

The SBIR program was still quite new and they have, to date, had little experience with the SBIR contracts in general and the Phase II contracts in particular. Obviously, having the potential of an opportunity to resubmit an application is something that would be helpful to know before selecting the mechanism for the application. Although the number of Primary disincentives were approximately equal to the number of Primary incentives, the positive merits of these incentives far outweigh the barriers presented by the disincentives. This is chiefly because the SBIR program enables a small business to successfully compete for federal R&D money. These awards frequently serve as the main source of initial funding for R&D work undertaken by individuals like myself. In addition to creating opportunities to develop new markets and jobs, "seed money" may result in stronger internal support.

SECONDARY INCENTIVES AND DISINCENTIVES

Secondary incentives and disincentives identified in this case study reveal that the federal government's support of the biomedical R&D innovation process has both social and economic implications for the entrepreneurial investigator and the corporation.

The social factors considered to be Secondary incentives and disincentives for the investigator and his or her organization are listed in Tables 5 and 6.

Table 5
Secondary Incentives and Disincentives to Innovation that have Social Implications for the Individual

Incentives

Opportunity to participate in application of own ideas.
Increased visibility in science community.

Disincentives

Bias of academic peer review against industry.
Six month time frame for total Phase I.

Table 6
Secondary Incentives and Disincentives to Innovation that have Social Implications for the Corporation

Incentives

Enhanced image.

Disincentives

Lack of peer review understanding of potential marketplace.

Application of One's Own Ideas

Principle among the factors considered to be Secondary social incentives are those related to prestige and the opportunity to participate in the application of one's own ideas for the betterment of society. The latter is an especially important Secondary social incentive in disease prevention and health promotion. This is because support has been almost entirely directed toward providing funds to states and local governments to promote voluntary application of healthier habits of living.

Increased Visibility

Because of the mandatory dual peer review system at NIH, a principal investigator's chance of acquiring funding is greater if he or she is recognized within the scientific community. Competitive federal support for new ideas through SBIR, enables the small business entrepreneur to acquire this necessary recognition.

Academic Bias Against Industry

The strongest Secondary social disincentive for both the small business entrepreneur and the small corporation is a perceived academic bias against industry. This bias may be the expression of an unwillingness to compete for the same resources. The bias is both formally and informally expressed. In the case of SBIR, House Subcommittee testimony by university-based researchers bears out this bias.

Six Month Time Frame for Phase I

Anyone interested in participating in the SBIR program needs to be aware of the 6 month time frame for Phase I projects. Any efforts to develop a prototype and test for feasibility will need to be well thought out and scaled down.

Enhanced Image

The ability to enhance the firm's image in the biomedical community through SBIR participation serves as an incentive for the corporation. A strong R&D image is an extremely important criterion in terms of corporate qualifications examined during the peer review process for other biomedical funding mechanisms. Name recognition associated with successful product or service development also enhances a firm's marketing "nitch."

Lack of Peer Review Understanding of Potential Market

The fact that almost all peer review group members belong to the academic community may also serve as a disincentive for the small business. If the reviewers do not know the competitive, for-profit environment, they may unwittingly make wrong decisions with regard to commercial viability. Additional ramifications of the emphasis on the use of university-based reviewers will be discussed in detail in the section titled, *Review of Summary Report of Technical Review Documents.*

SECONDARY ECONOMIC INCENTIVES AND DISINCENTIVES

Tables 7 and 8 present Secondary incentives and disincentives thought to have economic implications for the individual investigator and the corporation. Because there is considerable overlap these Secondary incentives and disincentives will be discussed together.

Ability to Obtain R&D funds

A firm's ability to compete successfully for SBIR awards is, in large part, dependent upon the credentials of the principal investigator. Under SBIR guidelines this individual must be with the firm at the time of award and during the conduct of the proposed project. "The Code of

Table 7
Secondary Incentives and Disincentives Thought to have Economic Implications for the Individual

---

Incentives

Ability to obtain R&D funds.
Potential for increased future income.

Disincentives

Long lag time between proposal submission and funding.
Fifty thousand dollar limit on Phase I projects.
Lack of corporate resources to complete the project.
Reviewer confusion over SBIR funding mechanism definitions.
Agency budgetary constraints for cancer related innovations.

Table 8
Secondary Incentives and Disincentives Thought to Have Financial Implications for the Corporation

---

Incentives

Increased future earnings.
Achievement of revenue growth objectives.
Achievement of profit objectives.
Availability of R&D funds.
Lack of capital risk.
Product ownership.

Disincentives

Lack of coverage of product by reimbursement policy.
Long delay from submission of proposal to funding.

Federal Regulations, Title 42, Part 52, defines a principal investigator as 'the single individual designated by the contractor or grantee in the application...who is responsible for the scientific and technical direction of the project'" (DHHS, 1985, p. 3).

Potential for Increased Future Income

Because government places great importance on the role of the principal investigator in the SBIR program, there is potential for his or her to receive financial recognition within the small business. This obviously serves as an incentive to the individual to produce winning proposals.

These incentives also work for the small firm as well. For if the individual is successful, the company will stand to increase future earnings, thus achieving its growth and profit objectives with little outlay or risk of it's own capital. In addition, the company maintains product ownership (Table 8).

As with the incentives, Primary disincentives were also thought to serve as Secondary economic disincentives. These have to do with budgetary constraints and the inability of the corporation to raise its own capital to complete Phase II activities.

Fifty Thousand Dollar Limit on Phase I Projects

A financial handicap to using the SBIR program was that the Phase I project had to be completed in less than 6 months with a maximum budget of $50,000. This limitation of time and money suggests that the company and the Principal Investigator need to be well organized and staffed prior to submitting the application. In that way, all would be ready to go as soon as the funding is made available. Any delay in completion of Phase I also will result in a longer funding gap between the end of Phase I and the beginning of Phase II.

For this case study the most significant secondary economic disincentive to participate in the SBIR program involved the impact of the dual peer review system.

Application of the Dual Peer Review Process to the SBIR

Access to multiple approved SBIR contract and grant proposals provided an opportunity to generalize about the impact of the dual peer review system on efforts to reach the commercialization step of the innovation process.

The task of analyzing the impact of the peer review system proved to be a difficult one. This was partly due to the administrative differences and similarities of the review process for the grants and contracts. An example of one of the differences is the selection and orientation of Peer Review Groups.

SELECTION AND ORIENTATION OF PEER REVIEW GROUPS

Conversations with NIH SBIR Program Administrators revealed that each uses a slightly different process to assemble members for the SBIR Peer Review Groups. According to the Health Sciences Administrator, Division of Research Grants,[4] the SBIR process follows that of all grants reviewed. The member selection is made using the following sources:

1. Curriculum vitae of individuals expressing an interest in serving in this capacity.
2. Individuals who have published extensively in the topic area.
3. DRG files containing names of individuals previously used for review groups.

For the SBIR program, at least one member of the 6 to 12 member group currently must be employed in private industry.

The Administrator for NIH sponsored SBIR Contracts stated that contract review groups are assembled by each division within the institutes.[5] Potential candidates are selected from lists of individuals recommended by the division scientists themselves. Review of prospective member credentials also are done within the respective divisions. Groups may vary from 6 to 12 members. It is not known whether any reviewers of the contract applications were associated with private industry.

Appendix A contains a copy of the materials provided to reviewers at the Review Group Member Orientation. These guidelines include an abbreviated description of the SBIR program, evaluation criteria for Phase I and Phase II review, confidentiality and conflict of interest information, as well as instructions for preparing Summary Report of Technical Review Statements. While the materials are scanty, they do contain information specific to the SBIR review process. They do not, however, emphasize those areas which differ from the traditional grants. These printed materials are the only instructions peer reviewers receive prior to evaluating SBIR proposals.

REVIEW OF SUMMARY REPORT OF TECHNICAL REVIEW DOCUMENTS

The analysis of the *Summary Report of Technical Review* documents involved the interpretation of the peer reviews themselves. Phase I reviews contained a minimum of five categorical comment sections: merit of the technical approach, qualifications of the proposed staff, product's commercial potential, adequacy of the research facilities, and cost. The Phase II reviews contained an additional category--progress made in Phase I. (Appendix C contains a sample document.)

To classify the types of peer reviewer comments received, each of the categories for six contract review statements was evaluated by comparing individual statements representing strengths against weaknesses. These statements were then classified as difficult to interpret in terms of overall technical merit, displayed lack of understanding of the purpose of the SBIR program or project, or were reasonable and acceptable.

A majority or minority opinion of the review group was not provided for any of the contract *Summary Report of Technical Review* documents. This made it impossible to know whether each of the statements listed represented one or more than one opinion. Therefore, the percentages were determined by giving equal weight to each statement.

The results of the evaluation are presented in Tables 9 and 10. Table 9 presents the evaluation made of the Summary Report of Technical Review Document categories covering technical merit, personnel qualifications, commercial potential, adequacy of developer facilities, and estimated costs. For this evaluation the total number of statements documenting strengths and weaknesses within each category were evaluated by whether they were predominately confusing, showed lack of understanding of SBIR Program or were reasonable acceptable.

Many of the categories contained contradictory statements concerning the strengths and weaknesses of the proposals as they related to the merits of the technical approach, qualifications of the proposed personnel, product commercial potential, and adequacy of the research facilities. The greatest number of contradictory statements were noted in the merits of the technical approach category. The next largest category, related to personnel classifications, was found primarily in the category of commercial potential. There was an almost even distribution between the percentage of comments judged to be contradictory and those thought to be reasonable and acceptable. Most of the reasonable and acceptable comments were related to adequacy of facilities and costs.

Figures 3 and 4 provide examples of reviewer comments by two of the three classifications; those which were confusing and those thought to show a lack of understanding of the program or project. Those judged to be confusing in terms of the overall impact of the statements on the technical score have been paired.

Analysis of the *Summary Report of Technical Review* for the one Phase I Grant project was much easier to interpret than those of the contracts. The critique consisted of a majority opinion and a minority opinion.

It was also possible to determine how many individuals made up the majority and how many the minority. A review of the Peer Review roster indicated the group was made-up of seven individuals affiliated with a university and only one member affiliated with a profit-oriented organization.

Table 9
Summary Report Document Categories for Six Contract Proposals

Category	Strengths	Weakness	Classification
Proposal 1			
Merit	7	10	Confusing
Personnel	2	4	Confusing
Potential	1	1	Lack Understanding
Facilities	1	1	Acceptable
Costs	1	1	Acceptable
Proposal 2			
Merit	4	4	Confusing
Personnel	1	1	Confusing
Potential	1	1	Confusing
Facilities	1	0	Acceptable
Proposal 3			
Merit	5	3	Acceptable
Personnel	1	0	Acceptable
Potential	2	3	Acceptable
Facilities	1	0	Acceptable
Cost	1	0	Acceptable
Proposal 4			
Progress	2	5	Acceptable
Merit	5	6	Lack Understanding
Personnel	3	3	Confusing
Potential	2	2	Confusing
Facilities	2	2	Confusing
Cost	1	0	Acceptable
Proposal 5			
Progress	5	7	Confusing
Merit	5	5	Confusing
Personnel	2	2	Confusing
Potential	4	3	Acceptable
Proposal 6			
Progress	2	5	Acceptable
Merit	4	5	Lack Understanding
Personnel	2	2	Confusing
Potential	1	2	Confusing
Facilities	1	1	Acceptable
Objectives	3	3	Lack Understanding

Table 10
Classification of the 28 Summary Report of Technical Review Document Categories

Number of Categories	Percent	Classification
12	43	Confusing
13	46	Appropriate
2	11	Lack of Understanding

In general, several barriers identified through the review of the *Summary Report of Technical Review* documents were related to a lack of sufficient communication by the government at several levels. First, the reviewers do not appear to have received enough instruction concerning the objectives of this special funding mechanism. In addition to the lack of understanding regarding copyright and patent issues, reviewers seemed to lose sight that SBIR projects were to be completed within six months of award, thereby expecting too much in the way of validation and testing.

DISCUSSION

Data collected from SBIR participating agencies by USGAO while this study was underway lend strong support to these findings. The first corroborating data involved an evaluation of federal agencies' procedures for making SBIR selections and awards (USGAO. October, 1985). In the USGAO report, the authors concluded that less than one-half of the twelve agencies participating in SBIR activities had awarded their Phase I contracts and grants within six months of receiving the

Strengths

Overall, the proposed staff appears to be excellent.

Weaknesses

The proposed programmer does not appear to have experience in developing assembly programs, or in programming a base function calculator.

****

Strengths

The investigators have experience in nutrition as well as computer related nutrition projects.

Weaknesses

The key personnel have no formal computer expertise.

****

Strengths

The tool is innovative and, if it can be validated, may have considerable commercial application.

Weaknesses

At this stage, the value of the project is still speculative.

****

Strengths

The proposed staff appears to have experience in hardware and software as well as health education.

Weaknesses

The proposed staff appear to be weak in nutrition education and evaluation expertise.

The computer staff appears to have limited formal training.

****

Strengths

The proposed PI appears to be well qualified to manage this project. She has adapted PECAN, written SAS macros, SAS/GRAPH, and has analysis experience.

Weaknesses

The Ph.D. degree of the PI is not relevant to the proposed work. She does not have much experience in programming.

Figure 3. Paired Summary Report statements considered to be confusing to interpret in terms of overall impact on on technical scores.

SBIR guidelines emphasize the retention of rights in data, copyrights and patents to inventions and technical data from the funded work.

"One reviewer recommended that the proposal is technically unacceptable because the offeror apparently required a copy protection to its product. This reviewer indicated that the proposal would be technically acceptable if the copy protection issue is dropped."

****

The SBIR solicitation states "It would be advantageous to develop user friendly programs for the personal computer using *existing* programs as models where ever possible."

"The proposed system is thought not to have technological innovation, and the quality would be too low for much commercial application."

"The proposed statistical package appears to have little scientific merit beyond what exists now."

****

Reviewer missed the purpose of the software development. Both the abstract and the Scope of Work carefully described the purpose of the software to be that of a "triage" for screening only.

"The correlation coefficients cited for calories, fat, and protein are not very encouraging compared to the 3-day diet diary."

****

"At this state, the value of the project is still speculative."

Figure 4. Examples of Summary Report statements thought to display lack of understanding of SBIR program or proposed project.

proposal. This was a goal established by SBA guidelines. A similar observation was presented in this analysis as a serious disincentive to beginning a project. Any proposed timely innovations with potential widespread commercial application run the risk of being done by someone else while waiting for a funding decision from the government.

In a second USGAO report (1987, July), the government provides information on small businesses participating in the SBIR program. Data contained in this report documented a 1986 survey conducted of 1406 of a total of 3241 projects in fiscal years 1983 to 1985 (study firm was not one of those selected to be sampled). Questionnaires queried about the SBIR project, firm's experiences with the SBIR program, and characteristics of the firm at which the project took place.

According to the USGAO survey (1987), almost all respondents considered their participation in the SBIR program to be worthwhile. The benefits companies reported were the ability to fund R&D work that was not being funded by another source and improving other products as a result of R&D work on the SBIR project.

Survey respondents echoed similar general satisfaction with the up-front administration of the SBIR program. In keeping with this study's findings, over one-half of the respondents expressed considerable dissatisfaction with the gap in funding between the end of Phase I award and the onset of Phase II support. The gap in funding varied by agency, and for the majority of the sampled projects, the gap ranged from 3 to 12 months.

USGAO attempted to obtain additional information regarding the funding gap issue from federal officials responsible for the SBIR program. They interviewed individuals at the Department of Energy (DOE), the Department of Defense (DOD), NSF and DHHS--the four agencies that accounted for 80 percent of all SBIR dollars in fiscal year 1985.

DHHS was not able to provide USGAO sufficient payment data to conduct a thorough funding pay analysis. However, USPHS officials indicated there were administrative practices that contributed to the funding gap. These were:

1. USPHS allows phase II proposals not selected for an award but judged meritorious to compete with other phase II proposals in a subsequent cycle within the same fiscal year. Thus, the proposals can be kept alive for as long as three review cycles.
2. USPHS allows SBIR firms up to three consecutive receipt dates following the end of phase I to submit their phase II grant proposals (i.e., if a company elected to submit its phase II proposal on the third receipt date, it would be almost a year from the time its phase I grant ended).
3. USPHS proposals that contain research to be performed on animal or human subjects are required to comply with federal regulations governing the filing of assurances of compliance with and obtaining the approval of appropriately constituted review committees within the applicant organization. (USGAO, 1987, July, p.46).

The results of this case study are similar to those USGAO findings with regard to the funding gap. The funding gap experienced here reflected the worst case scenario described to USGAO by the USPHS officials.

In terms of secondary factors, the major sources of frustration centered around a lack of standardized definitions. Innovation process definitions should be developed and provided to both the reviewers and the organizations proposing the innovations.

Without standardized definitions there will continue to be confusion between innovation in terms of "novelty" vs. innovation in terms of its use in the "innovation process." For example, in this study this lack of standardization resulted in a reviewer commenting that the touch screen microcomputer was not new. That is true; however, the successful application of the touch screen to a supermarket environment was new.

Another especially strong Secondary disincentive to participate in the biomedical technology process through the SBIR was the finding that few reviewers from the private sector are included in the review group. If merit evaluation of the proposed project is to be done through peer review, then the review groups should include more peers and fewer academic scientists who have spoken out publicly concerning their disapproval of the SBIR program (NCI's SBIR Awards, 1986).

Personal scores provided by reviewers ultimately determined how the proposal would fall along the "payline." Each of the scores represented the reviewer's personal evaluation of the merit of the project overall--a totally subjective process.

In situations where funding is scarce, these scores become a critical component in the review process. A single reviewer's misinterpretation of the SBIR Phase I objectives could result in project approval, but no funding.

Of the five NCI approved innovations in the study, the Estimate-it calculator was considered to have the greatest potential for success (See Appendix B for detailed description). The device was judged by the NCI program staff to be a potentially useful adjunct to self-monitoring activities required in behavior change. The field study supported this notion with the finding that it was easy to use and would be inexpensive to produce. Because the product had undergone a highly successful field testing, the NCI program office expressed an interest in including it in a large Women's Health Trial designed to reduce fat intake as a possible breast cancer preventive. Unfortunately this was not to become a reality, because the Board of Scientific Counselors was unable to over-ride the priority score assigned by the peer review group.

A comparison of the number of positive forces noted in the Estimate-it innovation with those identified in the literature for successful innovations indicated this could have been a successful product. These included:

1. Recognition of a technical opportunity for a timely improvement of an existing manual process. That is, it would be technically possible to inexpensively automate a tedious manual activity.
2. Recognition of the need for solving a dietary problem.
3. Availability of funding early in the innovation process.
4. Market analysis indicated a sizable potential market.
5. Prior demonstration of technical feasibility.
6. Technical entrepreneur championed the activity.

Despite the presence of these positive forces pulling for the innovation process, the project was blocked. The obvious question then became: "Why?"

There is a long standing argument about the extent to which R&D can be managed. The calculator case study suggests that even when a project appears to incorporate an overwhelming number of positive factors, there are limits to the extent to which the R&D can be managed. That is, despite the fact that the feasibility study was completed on time and within budget, that a business plan was developed, a market analysis was done, and venture capital was available-- the project was blocked.

For the Estimate-it project, lack of continued corporate support provided the final barrier to the innovation process. Our internal business management group was unprepared to provide financial support beyond that which was necessary to obtain Phase I seed money from the government.

The Estimate-it project was subsequently brought before the NCI Board of Scientific Counselors by NCI's Program Staff in an attempt to have the project funded from available discretionary money. This effort failed as well. The NCI program people recognized the potential value of this project to their own research efforts, but could not over-ride the priority score given it by the peer review group during the first round of review. Appendix D contains a copy of the letter received from NCI, which in effect, put the project in limbo for almost a year--a genuine disincentive for a profit-oriented company.

A small supporting grant was later offered to the firm by the University of California, Los Angeles, to produce fifty of the calculators for one of their research projects. Management decided that it did not want to go forward until a final decision was made on the pending Phase II application. Once again the project was blocked.

The barriers described here have been observed by other SBIR Phase I developers as well (Innovation Development Institute, 1986). rather than an end in itself, a Phase I project must be designed as an integral part of a project for which the company assumes a long term commitment.

Table 11 presents a summary of the Primary and Secondary Incentives and Disincentives identified in this case study. In general, participating in the SBIR program is worthwhile. Small firms such as the one in this study, receive (a) financial rewards, (b) new opportunity to do R&D work for the government, and (c) possibility for commercial sale of SBIR results.

Although SBIR generally receives high marks, there are facets of the program that are discouraging. The participant needs to take time to personally identify the character and force of the Secondary Incentives and Disincentives. If he or she does not, there is apt to be a tendency to become sufficiently frustrated to decide to withdraw.

The consequences of withdrawal manifest themselves as a widening gap between basic research discoveries and their practical application. This innovation gap is now being addressed by the Committee of Science, Space, and Technology. Factors being examined include the environment for innovation and creativity, the level and forces of R&D funding, and the improvement of technology transfer.

In summary, the availability of financial support, from whatever source, emerged as an important requirement in the innovation process. Funding issues, in turn, are directly linked to the manner in which the peer review process is applied to the SBIR mechanism.

These potential barriers to innovation underscore the need for a technical entrepreneur in the innovation process. The technical entrepreneur provides the necessary driving force. Without a product champion to persist in spite of problems and setbacks, the innovation will most likely be tabled or blocked. This conclusion supports the results of previous studies (Schon, 1967).

Table 11
Summary of Primary and Secondary Incentives and Disincentives to
Participate in the Innovation Process

Incentives			
Primary	Sponsor	Individual	Developer
Generous R&D funding		x	x
Contracting policy			x
Patents/copyrights			x
Lobbying			x
Continuous funding cycle		x	x
Secondary			
Application of ideas		x	
Increased visibility		x	
Enhanced image			x
Increased future earnings		x	x
Achieve growth objectives			x
Achieve profit objectives			x
Available R&D funds		x	x
Lack of capital risk		x	x
Product ownership			x
Disincentives			
Primary			
Lobby	x	x	x
Low appropriations	x	x	x
No administrative support	x	x	
No external/internal funds		x	
Incomplete information		x	x
Secondary			
Peer review bias			x
Six month time frames		x	x
Marketplace information			x
No product reimbursement			x
Funding lag time		x	x
$50 thousand Phase I limit		x	x
No corporate resources		x	x
Reviewer understanding of SBIR		x	x
Agency budget constraints		x	x

CHAPTER VII NOTES

[1] Specific dates are published in USPHS *Omnibus Solicitation.*

[2] In accordance with federal regulation 45 CFR Part 74, no profit or fee will be provided to for-profit organizations through grants.

[3] NIH describes a R&D contract as an attempt to apply and develop the results of basic research through the negotiation of research and development contracts with qualified organizations to investigate or perform a directed scientific project with a well-defined work scope. Generally, the initiative for undertaking the research, design, direction, and methodology for the project originates within the NIH. Such initiatives are advertised in the *NIH Guide for Grants and Contracts* and the *Commerce Business Daily.*

[4] Information supplied in an interview, May 14, 1987.

[5] Information supplied in an interview, April 17, 1987.

VIII

Conclusions and Recommendations

The Comptroller General's 1985 report identified medical technology as one of 31 key health care cost containment issues. Problems related to the cost of medical technology result from the high priority that Americans accord to medical services compared to other means of improving health and to the premature adoption of medical advances.

If we are to deal effectively with the biomedical technology cost issue, we need a comprehensive understanding of the biomedical technology innovation process. For if the process can be better understood, then those conditions favoring desirable innovation can be promoted and accelerated. Conversely, ineffective or inappropriate innovations such as life-sustaining therapies for dying patients or unnecessary use of pharmaceuticals can be blocked.

Robert J. Blendon, Senior Vice President at the Robert Wood Johnson Foundation, suggests a number of critical policy choices may emerge in the mid-1990s given the current forces at work in the U.S. health care system (1986). To those concerned primarily with costs, proposals such as the rationing of high cost equipment and medical procedures and limiting the availability of these procedures to the elderly will need to be considered. Other proposals might involve substantially delaying government approval of new expensive technologies and transplants.

To organizations concerned with formulating health policy, an appreciation of the biomedical innovation process offers the hope of ameliorating some of these problems before they become serious. In this study the SBIR program at NIH served as a means to document factors and/or activities experienced while attempting to participate in the biomedical innovation process. Through the consideration of these

89

incentives and disincentives to participate, it also was possible to describe some of the health-care related ramifications of the federal government's pluralistic approach to technology policy.

The review of the literature presented in Chapters I through V, demonstrated that the federal government plays a major role in the biomedical technology innovation process. These chapters also demonstrated that concerns about policies and funding priorities for the U.S. biomedical research base cannot be separated from scientific, technological, economic, sociological, political, and institutional factors.

FEDERAL INVOLVEMENT IN BIOMEDICAL R&D

While opinions vary concerning many aspects of federal involvement in health care, there is general agreement that government should (a) sponsor basic research, (b) control potential negatives of technological activities, and (c) sponsor technologies that are in the public interest, but not alone well suited to free enterprise activities. There also is agreement that the government should attempt to ensure no single private concern makes undue profit from publicly funded research.

In the biomedical technology area, NIH has the primary responsibility for these governmental functions. The role of this federal medical research and development component, with respect to medical technology innovation, is multiple, varied, and in a constant state of flux. It is a dynamic environment because it depends upon a variety of interrelating or interdependent functions which themselves are changing.

NIH also fits into many positions within the biomedical technology innovation process because the federal government is a major researcher, a major research supporter, and a major consumer of medical technology. As the federal government's principle R&D facility, NIH serves as a major resource for advancing biomedical and other health-related technologies. It also collaborates with other agencies, universities, industry, and state and local government in both its research and technology transfer activities. Within the innovation process, NIH is directly involved in the discovery, development, evaluation and assessment steps. New technologies or applications of existing technologies are tracked by following basic biomedical and behavioral research. The evaluation and testing of such identified technologies are frequently conducted through the support of clinical trials and patenting or licensing procedures. Scientific merit is the primary criteria for judging whether a project should be supported.

The latter steps of the innovation process, which include formal technology assessment, technology transfer, information dissemination and promotion of the general application of research findings are handled through consensus development conferences, assessment reports, task force reports, workshops, and review articles. NIH describes its diffusion activities as: supporting clearing houses, development and distribution of scientific publications for lay audiences, state-of-the-art consensus conferences, and collaboration with the private sector in the conduct of clinical trials.

In 1982, NIH became more active in influencing the broad application of selected R&D research. This involvement was related to the passage of SBDA legislation. SBDA was designed to encourage innovations primarily by requiring federal agencies to award portions of their research funds to small businesses through SBIR procurement programs. The act mandates a three-phase approach for this program: an initial phase to demonstrate feasibility of a proposed project, a second phase to carry out the most promising Phase I projects, and a third phase to pursue commercial applications through non-federal dollars.

The SBDA legislation, which affects multiple agencies, mandates a uniform simplified format for operating the SBIR program and provides guidelines for minimizing the regulatory burden for firms participating in the program. SBIR projects must be performed under funding agreements (contract, grant, or cooperative agreement) between a small firm and a federal agency.

While agencies are required to follow uniform policies established for the SBIR program, they are allowed considerable flexibility in operating their individual programs to suit their own organizational needs. Agencies, for example, may determine SBIR research topics and may exercise discretion in selecting and evaluating projects, proposals, selecting awardees and administrating funding agreements for SBIR projects.

At NIH, the SBIR program was merged into the legislated peer review process. All Phase I and Phase II applications are evaluated and judged on a competitive basis. Each application is subjected to a peer review process involving two sequential steps. The first step is performed by a peer review group composed of non-federal scientists selected for their competence in particular scientific fields. The task of the peer review group is to evaluate the application for scientific and technical merit. The second level of review is made by the national advisory board of the awarding component to which the application is assigned.

Depending upon the size of the agency budget, a payline is also determined. For example, in 1987, no NCI awards were made to grantees whose priority scores exceeded 170 on a scale of 1 to 500. As funding is determined by the point score given to the approved project by the peer review group, not all approved applications are automatically funded.

PEER REVIEW IMPLICATIONS

While it is recognized any company interested in participating in SBIR must make come financial commitment to the program, the organization's success often is heavily dependent upon the way the agency handles its R&D related funding. This case study demonstrated that NIH provides numerous incentives to participate in the development of biomedical technology innovations. The majority of these incentives fall at the front end of the innovation process. The results of this study also suggest a major negative influence on the latter stages is directly related to peer review impact on the promotion of scientific results into a form the health care marketplace will consider useful.

At NIH, all proposals are subjected to the same review process; be they basic research, applied research, or evaluative research. This means that applications undergo a legislated dual peer review process. The first step is performed by a group composed primarily of non-federal scientists selected for their competence in a particular scientific field. These individuals provide a rating which determines where the application will fall along an NIH established payline.

The data evaluating the peer review process from the perspective of SBIR, suggests the direct application of this legislated peer review system contributes substantially to many of the delays in bringing federally funded scientific discoveries to the marketplace. This, in part, is due to differences between the SBIR proposal format and traditional grant applications and contract proposals. For example, SBIR proposals carry a 25 page limitation and frequently contain novel or unproven methodologies. Feasibility studies, by their very nature, carry an element of risk and uncertainty as to their outcome. Peer review, though considered essential to ensure quality science, appears to be skeptical of radical or "unproved" topics.

The peer review issue was addressed in Chapters I through V and, more recently, was discussed at a field hearing in Boston, Massachusetts. (NIH Officials, December 14, 1987). At this meeting, the NIH Deputy Director noted the peer review system has come under criticism as an "old-boys network" of scientists favoring East Coast private universities and western state schools. Research-intensive institutions, because of their meritocracy, also have an advantage. The Deputy Director stated that an NIH panel is studying peer review issues including whether the panels, in fact, do discourage high risk research.

Reluctance of review committees to approve novel ideas is very problematic for those interested in prevention innovation, as frequently there is insufficient data to quantify the benefits of prevention (excluding immunizations) in advance. This poses something of a dilemma as necessary data cannot be acquired if the projects do not receive funding.

The peer review system also appeared to act as a barrier to the commercialization process, in that peer reviewers seemed to experience difficulty in dealing with proprietary and commercialization issues.

POSSIBILITIES FOR CHANGING THE MANNER
IN WHICH SBIR IS HANDLED AT NIH

Promote Familiarization with Commercialization

Review panel make-up and the examples of individual reviewer comments found in the *Summary Report of Technical Review* documents for this study, suggest that the review groups should include more scientists familiar with both research and commercialization procedures. This would help to ensure that those engaged in producing the raw materials from which technological innovations result, will themselves have some appreciation for the down-stream use of scientific outcomes.

Greater use of entrepreneurial scientists on review groups would also help reduce the confusion regarding business development and product development. The SBIR program does not support market research or business development. That is the purpose of venture capital, government guarantees and direct loans. Rather, SBIR objectives center around encouraging the conversion of basic research in important scientific areas into technological innovation and commercial applications for its potential economic benefits to the nation. SBIR is not in competition with basic research. It is an extension of it.

Greater Use of Demonstration Projects

SBIR also complements the efforts of OMAR in the assessment and dissemination steps of the biomedical technology innovation process. As the nation's principal medical R&D component, NIH is directly and increasingly involved in assessing and, where appropriate, promoting use of the growing list of new health care technologies. So long as NIH funds the technology development and through OMAR, recommends what technologies should be reimbursable, NIH will be in a position to influence which technologies will be incorporated into the health care system.

As prevention is a national goal, the government should consider the incorporation of successful NIH SBIR prevention related products in OMAR demonstration projects. Such an approach would serve to enhance the biomedical technology innovation process by demonstrating the value of prevention technologies. Without formal support for prevention technology innovations, the bulk of federal resources will continue to go to biomedical technology acute care innovations.

In determining what research programs the government should support, the question should be whether the gain in health is a reasonable return for the resources expended. If this is the test applied to acute care, it should also be applied to prevention.

Review Funding Issues

In the last few years, the entire biomedical research community has become increasingly uneasy about the lack of stability of research funding (USGAO, 1987, March). For a SBIR participant such as myself, instability of funding also was a primary Disincentive to participate in the biomedical technology innovation process.

In this case, the absence of stability and predictability of federal support was the principal barrier to the production of the Estimate-it calculator. Overall, the on-again, off-again process was not only detrimental to the innovations themselves, it was destructive of research morale and efficiency. It also interfered with long-range corporate planning efforts.

Similar sentiments were expressed by the USGAO survey respondents (USGAO, 1987, July), who listed the following problems:

1. The long gap between Phase I and II made it impossible to maintain continuity of research and personnel.
2. It was difficult to stop work after Phase I funding ended and start up again when Phase II funding began. The work had to be continued at a great financial hardship to the company.
3. The time between the completion of Phase I and start of Phase II created a great disorder in the allocation of resources and personnel.
4. The gap in funding between Phase I and Phase II caused a severe loss of momentum.

5. The delay between Phase I and Phase II is a burden on any company, especially a small business. It is also an extremely inefficient use of personnel since the funding gap is often twice or more the length of the total Phase I program.
6. The slow timing of the funding, particularly between the end of the Phase I and the beginning of the Phase II, is problematic. For example, when research is going well and strong, it is unfortunate to have to end it when the Phase I money runs out. Also it is difficult to plan to have available the capable technical staff when and if the Phase II funding is granted.

Many of the observations are directly attributable to the federal budget process including:

1. Constraints on oversight and long term planning created by the annual budget cycle.
2. A program/agency approach to R&D budgeting that limits interagency comparisons by research field or discipline.
3. Restrictions on appropriations that limit stability in multi-year funding of research.

The annual budget cycle, combined with constraints on agencies to limit the time period over which funds from a specified fiscal year appropriation can be obligated, causes uncertainty and gaps in continuity of research support. Uncertainty created by the annual budget appropriation cycle and constraints limiting the time duration of obligations prohibit agency program managers from assuring individual investigators continuous, stable support over a period of years. In the case of SBIR, the guarantee is for six months.

USGAO's SBIR statistics indicated that this situation is not unique to this study (1987, July). Their data showed there was an agency wide average lag time of about eight months between receipt of the last Phase I payment and the first Phase II funds. For DHHS, this lag is augmented by the low proportion of Phase II awards made; DHHS funding only an average of one third of the applications.

Interim Funding

To minimize both funding interruptions between Phase I and Phase II projects and delays in contractor Phase II award notification, NIH should consider both an early decision program for Phase II and possible provision of interim funding to all Phase II contractors between phases. Such a program currently exists within the DOE and was evaluated by USGAO. According to USGAO, the DOE early decision program and its provision of interim funding has achieved the greatest success in reducing the funding gap (USGOA, 1987, July). These programs are possible within DOE, because the agency makes the determination as to the "outstanding nature" of the Phase I research.

These suggestions could not be implemented at NIH unless a special review structure was developed for SBIR within NIH. It is recommended that NIH should undertake such a review to determine what steps may be taken to improve the rate at which projects are reviewed and funded.

STATUS OF SBIR IN 1993

In the five years since this study was conducted, the SBIR program has continued to provide much needed support to small business researchers engaged in biomedical innovation research. For example, in Fiscal Year 1992, which was the tenth year of funding under the SBIR program, the Department of Health and Human Services (DHHS) made a total of 777 competing grant and contract awards, of which 619 were for Phase I and 158 for Phase II. The amount awarded by the DHHS for all SBIR awards, including the competing awards above, totaled almost $102 million. Funding from NIH accounted for $99 million of the total amount. NCI provided about $16 million for SBIR grants and $2 million for SBIR contracts. One hundred fifty-nine Phase I and 16 Phase II grants along with four Phase I and six Phase II contracts were funded by NCI.

While disincentives such as the long gap between submission of application, review process, and funding; the lack of available funding to continue the project between Phase I and II; and uncertainty concerning the amount of funding available from one fiscal year to another still exist, the program continues to   offer unparalleled advantages to the small business.

In Fiscal Year 1992, Public Law 102-564, the "Small Business Research and Development Enhancement Act of 1992," was signed by the President October 28, 1992.   The legislation authorized the continuation of the SBIR program through fiscal year 2000. It also calls for federal government agencies that award research grants and contracts to set aside greater percentages of money for small businesses and to improve the participation of women-owned and socially and economically disadvantaged small businesses in the program. Under the new guidelines agencies with extramural research budgets over $100 million must increase the set aside for small business from 1.25 percent to 2.5 percent by 1997. This is good news for all entrepreneurial researchers who are interested in biomedical technology transfer and are associated with small businesses, as about 97 percent of the SBIR activity of the Department of Health and Human Services takes place at the NIH.

Glossary of Terms

Biomedical Technology. Biomedical technology includes the drugs, devices, and medical and surgical procedures used in medical care, and the organizational and support systems within which such care is delivered. It may also be categorized by its purpose; including prevention, diagnosis, treatment, and rehabilitation.

Contract. A contract is an award instrument establishing a binding legal procurement relationship between a funding agency and the recipient, obligating the latter to furnish an end product or service and binding the agency to provide payment therefor.

Decisive Event. Selected from among the significant events, a decisive event is an occurrence that provides a major and essential impetus to the innovation.

Development. Development is that part of the history of the innovation involving the design of a feasible prototype and ends with the first commercial application and use.

Disincentive. Also understood to be a barrier, it consists of an action or condition that hampers the advancement of an innovation through the technological innovation process leading towards successful commercialization.

Dual Peer Review Process. All grant and contract applications submitted to NIH are subjected to a peer review process involving two sequential steps, both of which are required by law. The first step is performed by the Initial Review Groups (IRG), composed primarily of non-federal scientists selected for their competence in particular scientific fields. The task of the IRGs is to evaluate applications for scientific and technical merit. For those applications recommended for approval, the reviewers provide a rating. The second level of review is made by the National Advisory Council, or the board of the awarding component to which the application is assigned. Applications recommended for approval are not automatically funded.

Grant. A grant is a financial assistance mechanism whereby money and/or direct assistance is provided to carry out approved activities.

Incentive. An action or condition which facilitates the advancement of emerging technology innovation through the technological innovation process leading toward successful commercialization.

Innovation. A technical innovation is a complex activity which proceeds from the conception of a new idea [as a means of solving a problem] to a solution of the problem, and then to the actual utilization of a new item of economic or social value.

Non-technical Event. A non-technical event is a social or political occurrence outside the fields of science and technology.

Request for Application (RFA). A Request for Application is a government solicitation requesting applications for financial assistance to carry out activities in an area that is of general interest to the government.

Request for Proposal (RFP). A Request for Proposal is a government solicitation requesting proposals from qualified firms to provide specific end products or services.

Research, or Research and Development. Research and Development is any activity which is: (a) a systematic, intensive study directed toward greater knowledge or understanding of the subject studied; (b) a systematic study directed specifically toward applying new knowledge to meet a recognized need; or (c) a systematic application of knowledge toward the production of useful materials, devices, and systems or methods, including design, development and improvement of prototypes and new processes to meet specific requirements.

Significant Event. A significant event is an occurrence judged by the investigator to encapsulate an important activity encountered in the innovation process.

Small Business. A small business is any concern that at the time of an SBIR award (a) is independently owned and operated, is not dominant in the field of operation in which it is proposing and has its principal place of business located in the United States; (b) is at least 51 percent owned or, at least 51 percent of its voting stock is owned by United States citizens or lawfully admitted permanent resident aliens; and (c) has a number of employees not exceeding 500. Business concerns include but are not limited to any individual, partnership, corporation, joint venture, association or cooperative.

Summary Report of Technical Review. A summary report documents the evaluation of an application by the initial review group and conveys the group's recommendations to the awarding component and its council.

Technology. Technology is the systematic application of scientific or other organized knowledge to practical tasks.

Appendix A

[Provided by NIH--February, 1986]
REVIEW GROUP MEMBERS' ORIENTATION
SMALL BUSINESS INNOVATION RESEARCH (SBIR) PROGRAM
SMALL BUSINESS INNOVATION DEVELOPMENT ACT OF 1982
(P. L. 97-219)

P. L. 97-219, an amendment to the Small Business Act, requires the agencies of the Public Health Service (PHS) and certain other federal agencies to set aside a specified amount of their research and development (R&D) budgets for a Small Business Innovation Research (SBIR) Program. The purpose of this legislation is to:

1. Stimulate technological innovation.
2. Use small business to meet federal research and development needs.
3. Increase private sector commercialization of innovations derived from federal research and development.
4. Foster and encourage participation by minority and disadvantaged persons in technological innovation.

The Small Business Innovation Development Act is intended to promote technological innovation within the American small business community and thereby create jobs, augment industrial productivity, increase competition, and spur growth.

THE PHS SBIR PROGRAM

For purposes of the SBIR Program, "research" or "research and development (R&D) is defined as any activity which is: (a) a systematic, intensive study directed toward greater knowledge or

103

understanding of the subject studied; (b) a systematic study directed specifically toward applying new knowledge to meet a recognized need; or (c) a systematic application of knowledge toward the production of useful materials, devices, and systems or methods, including design, development and improvement of prototypes and new processes to meet specific requirements.

The SBIR Program consists of the following three phases:

Phase I (R43): establishes the technical merit and feasibility of proposed research or R&D efforts that may ultimately lead to commercial products or services, and to determine the quality of performance of the small business awardee organization. Awards normally may not exceed $50,000 (both direct and indirect costs) for a period normally not to exceed 6 months.

Phase II (R44): is to continue the research or R&D effort initiated in Phase I which are likely to result in commercial products or services. Funding shall be based on the results of Phase I and the scientific and technical merit of the Phase II applications. Only Phase I awardees are eligible to apply for Phase II funding. Phase II awards normally may not exceed $500,000 (including both direct and indirect costs) for a period normally not to exceed 2 years.

Phase III: small businesses are to pursue with private capital the commercialization of the results of R&D funded in Phases I and II, or a Federal agency may award non-SBIR funded contracts for products or processes intended for use by the U. S. Government.

The following definitions of approval, disapproval and deferral will be used in the review of SBIR applications.

Approval: the application is of sufficient merit to be worthy of support based on the relevant review criteria. The vote for approval is equivalent to a recommendation that a grant be awarded provided sufficient funds are available.

Disapproval: the application is not of sufficient merit, or for other stated reasons (e.g., gravely hazardous or unethical procedures are involved), not worthy of support.

Deferral (applicable only to Phase II): the application may be deferred because of insufficient information to make a recommendation, for additional information or for a project site visit.

REVIEW OF PHASE I

Since Phase I is to be a technical feasibility study, reviewers should not expect the application to provide data establishing feasibility of the project.

The evaluation criteria for Phase I review are as follows:

1. Scientific and technical merit of the proposed approach.
2. Qualifications of the principal investigator, supporting staff and consultants.
3. Appropriateness of the budget requested.
4. Adequacy and suitability of the facilities and research environment.
5. For administrative use by NIH staff, please comment on the potential of the proposed research for commercial application.

The recommended action and the priority score will be based on an assessment of the scientific and technical merit of the application, but not on commercial potential.

In accordance with the Code of Federal Regulations, Title 42, Part 52, the principal investigator of a research project is a "single individual, designated by the grantee in the grant application and approved by the Secretary, who is responsible for the scientific and technical direction of the project". "Consultants" from academia cannot provide the scientific/technical direction for the project unless they are in the employ of the small business *more* than one-half time.

The six-month budget will be examined and modified, if necessary. Amounts over the prescribed level will be handled by BID staff.

The resources and environment will be assessed.

If human subjects are involved, the adequacy of human subject protection will be assessed.

The authenticity and structure of the small business, the relationship of the key personnel to the small business and to other institutions, etc., are administrative matters. Comments will be appropriate in Administrative Notes, but these factors will not affect the scientific and technical merit evaluation.

REVIEW OF PHASE II

The definition of approval, disapproval and deferral, given above, will be used.

The evaluation criteria for Phase II review are as follows:

1. Degree to which the Phase I objectives were met and feasibility demonstrated.
2. Scientific, technical, and/or public health impacts of the problem or opportunity and anticipated benefits if Phase II research is successful.
3. The adequacy of the Phase II objectives and methodology for addressing the problem or opportunity.
4. The technical merit of the proposed research with special emphasis on innovation and/or originality.
5. The qualifications of the principal investigator, supporting staff and consultants.
6. The reasonableness of the budget requested for the proposed.
7. The adequacy and suitability of the facilities and research environment.

For administrative use by the NIH staff, please comment on:

The potential of the proposed research for commercial application. The recommended action and the priority score will be based on an assessment of the results of the Phase I effort (as reflected in the final report) and the technical merit of the proposed Phase II research. Expectations of Phase I results should take into consideration the brevity of the Phase I grant period (six months).

In accordance with the Code of Federal Regulations, Title 42, Part 52, the principal investigator of a research project is "a single individual, designated by the grantee in the grant application and approved by the Secretary, who is responsible for the scientific and technical direction of the project". "Consultants" from academia cannot provide the scientific/technical direction for the project unless they are in the employ of the small business *more* than one-half time.

The budget will be examined and modified, if necessary. Amounts and term of support over the prescribed level will be handled by BID staff.

If a study section believes that a Phase II project can be accomplished within a shorter period of time than proposed by the principal investigator, it may reduce the amount and period of support accordingly. The resources and environment will be assessed.

Biohazards should be assessed.

If human subjects are involved, the adequacy of human subject protection will be assessed.   If animals are involved, the adequacy of the care and use of animals will be assessed.

The authenticity and structure of the small business, the relationship of the key personnel to the small business and to other institutions, etc., are administrative matters. Comments will be appropriate in Administrative Notes, but these factors will not affect the scientific merit evaluation.

CONFIDENTIALITY

All materials pertinent to the applications being reviewed are privileged communications prepared for use only by consultants and NIH staff and should not be shown to or discussed with other individuals. Consultants are requested to leave all review materials with the Executive Secretary at the conclusion of the review meeting.

Under no circumstances should consultants advise either investigators or their organizations or anyone else of recommendations or discuss the review proceedings with them. The investigator may be led into unwise actions on the basis of premature or erroneous information. Such advice also represents an unfair intrusion into the privileged nature of the proceedings and invades the privacy of applicants as well as consultants serving on review committees. A breach of confidentiality could (1) result in disclosure of trade secrets or other proprietary information (commercial as well as financial) and (2) deter qualified consultants from serving on review committees and inhibit those who do so from engaging in free and full discussion of recommendations.

CONFLICT OF INTEREST

A. *A study section may not review an application in which*:

1. One of its members, or the member's spouse, parent, or child, is the principal investigator or is listed on the budget page in any capacity.
2. One of its members is an owner or officer in the organization submitting the application.
3. A member's close professional associate is the principal investigator or is responsible for conducting any portion of the planned research. The exact determination of how close the professional association must be to be considered a conflict of interest is a matter of judgment. The decision will be based on the recency, frequency, and strength of the working relationship between the member and the associates.

B. *Reviewers must leave the room during the review of an application*:

1. Involving their own organization. In the case of organizations with multiple sites geographically separated, the term "own organization" includes the entire system in which the member is an employee, or with which the member is negotiating or has any arrangement concerning prospective employment.
2. Submitted by an organization in which the member has a financial interest. This includes holding stock in or serving as a consultant for the organization.
3. If the member's presence would give the appearance of a conflict of interest.

COMMUNICATIONS WITH INVESTIGATORS

There should be no direct communications between members of review groups and investigators. Reviewers' requests for additional information and telephone inquiries or correspondence should be directed to the executive secretary who will handle all such communications.

GUIDE FOR ASSIGNED REVIEWERS' PRELIMINARY COMMENTS ON SMALL BUSINESS INNOVATION RESEARCH GRANT APPLICATIONS

Please use the following guidelines when preparing written comments on SBIR applications.

DESCRIPTION. Clearly and concisely describe the objectives and procedures of the application. Use the abstract on page 2 of the application unless inappropriate. *Do not make evaluative statements in this section.*

CRITIQUE. Scientific Merit. Do not repeat the description in this section. Provide a comprehensive evaluation of the strengths and weaknesses of the application, including the significance and innovativeness of the proposed research, the rationale for the study, the logic of the aims, and the adequacy of the procedures. For Phase II applications assess the degree to which Phase I objectives were met and feasibility demonstrated.

INVESTIGATORS. Assess the competence of the principal investigator(s) and key staff to conduct the proposed research, including their academic qualifications, research experiences, productivity, and any special attributes.

RESOURCES AND ENVIRONMENT. Discuss any special aspects of the facilities and equipment. Comment on the availability of essential laboratory, clinical, animal, computer, or other resources.

BUDGET. Determine whether all items of the budget are realistic and justified in terms of the aims and methods. Provide adequate justification for each suggested modification in amount.

OTHER CONSIDERATIONS

Overlap. Identify any apparent scientific or budgetary overlap with active or pending support.

Potential Commercial Application (if applicable). Comment on the potential of the proposed research for commercial application.

Involvement of Human Subjects.

Exemptions Claimed. Evaluate the appropriateness of the claimed exemptions, or

No Exemptions Claimed. Assess the appropriateness of the subject population. Explain any potential physical, psychological, social, or legal risks to individuals who are participating as subjects in research, development, or related activities. Describe the procedures for protecting against or minimizing such risks, and discuss whether the risks as reasonable in relation to the anticipated benefits to subjects and

the importance of the knowledge that may reasonably be expected to result. Assess the adequacy of the consent procedures.

Animal Welfare. If vertebrate animals are to be used in the project, discuss the appropriateness of the choice of species and numbers involved, and the justification for their use. Assess whether the animals will receive proper care and maintenance, and will not suffer unnecessary discomfort, pain, or injury.

Hazardous Materials and Procedures. Describe any potentially hazardous materials and procedures and whether the proposed protection provided by the investigator will be adequate.

SUMMARY AND RECOMMENDATION

Provide an overall evaluation of the strengths and weaknesses of the application and a recommendation of approval or disapproval.

NOTE: Under the Privacy Act of 1974, principal investigators may have access, upon request, to documents generated during the review of their grant applications. You do not have to sign written comments, and your comments will destroyed after being incorporated into the summary statement. In the event that your comments must be made available to a principal investigator you will be promptly notified by NIH staff.

Appendix B

[The following are excerpts from a final report submitted to NCI, DCPC, NIH, in fulfillment of a requirement for contract number N43-CN-55515.]

ESTIMATE-IT CALCULATOR

The innovation demonstration project described here, the single purpose calculator for use in encouraging long-term adherence to diets thought to reduce cancer risk, is traced from its original concept in 1982, through the field testing of a prototype in 1986.

The prototype device consists of a Radio Shack Pocket Computer PC-3 with 4K of memory. This instrument called "Estimate-it," calculates and records twenty-four hour aggregate data for calorie and fat intake. These estimates are derived from a table of 34 food groups similar to those developed in earlier research (Gardner et al., 1985).

The calculator utilizes a numeric key pad and three function keys for respondent input, and a character screen for displaying messages to the subject. The system also has an interface capable of uploading input data for analysis by researchers.

SOCIAL SIGNIFICANCE

Issues related to nutrition and food consumption involve complex interactions among social, cultural, economic, and physiological factors. Providing strategies to remedy nutrition problems has been a part of nearly every culture. Throughout history, many methods have been tried for modifying dietary habits. Between them, the popular press and the medical profession have probably suggested several hundred. These have been based mainly on drugs and diets, with some hypnosis, psychotherapy, and surgery thrown in. Most of these methods

113

work spectacularly for a few people, but not very well for most. Even among those people whose diets change, most later regress to their former eating patterns (Ferguson, 1976).

In the U.S., interest in diet and health has never been greater. A recent Harris survey indicated that 71 percent of all Americans believe that better nutrition is necessary for better health (Omenn & Simopoulous, 1982). A 1980 study done by the Food Marketing Institute found that Americans are more concerned about their fat and cholesterol intake than ever before (Yankelovich, Shelly & White, Inc., 1980). Consumer research by *Good Housekeeping* magazine has shown that the use of "lite" products skyrocketed in 1983 and 1984, and that interest in fiber and calcium has increased markedly since 1984 (McNutt, 1986).

In addition to these recent changes in food habits and attitudes, Americans are exercising more and smoking less. Furthermore, greater steps are being taken today to control hypertension than in previous years. It is also interesting to note that death rates from major killer diseases such as coronary heart disease (CHD), are continually declining year after year (Belloc & Breslow, 1972; Stamler, 1978; Stamler, 1982; Walker, 1977; DHEW, 1979).

In times when interest in diet and health is at its peak, there is tremendous need to provide sound nutrition information to the public. Although Americans are bombarded with an abundance of information about diet and nutrition, ironically they are still confused about what constitutes the "ideal" diet. Clearly, there is a need to provide assistance in guiding the way to better eating.

HISTORICAL ACCOUNT

There is increasing evidence that health-promoting nutritional behaviors play a vital role in the health status of the U.S. population (Belloc & Breslow, 1972). The government has served as a highly effective outlet to promote desirable dietary changes (National Research Council, 1983). A major government effort which has provided valuable information on the "diet-disease" connection is the Framingham Study (Dawber, Meadors & Moore, 1951; Dawber,

Moore & Mann, 1957; Dawber & Kannel, 1958; Kannel & Gordon, 1969).

Since 1949, this project has investigated the various risk factors involved in the development of CHD. The primary area of study focused on the effect of dietary fats and cholesterol on serum cholesterol levels. Another study which has attempted to answer the "diet-disease" question is the National Heart, Lung, and Blood Institute (NHLBI) funded Multiple Risk Factor Intervention Trial (MRFIT-Multiple Risk Factor Intervention Trial Research Group, 1982). Almost 13,000 men at risk of heart attack participated in this seven year program. Spontaneous, that is unexplained, behavioral changes were noted in both experimental and control groups, even though the latter group was not given special treatment to help modify their diets, stop smoking, and control their blood pressure. Lower mortality rates from CHD were also noted in both groups. Spontaneous decreases in CHD mortality rates have been observed in a number of other intervention programs as well (Farquhar et al., 1977; Fortmann, Williams, Hulley, Haskell & Farquhar, 1981; Maccohy, Farquhar, Wood & Alexander, 1977; Smith, Nelson & O'Hara, 1982; Stamler, 1982).

Nutrition and cancer are currently being viewed from two perspectives. The first is the role that nutrients play in the initiation or the induction of cancer. The second is in the use of nutritional support as an adjunct in the biological treatment of cancer.

An example of the first perspective is intake of dietary fat which correlates with increased prevalence of cancer of the breast, colon, and prostate. As animal models have shown that diets high in fat provide a favorable environment for the growth of tumors, it is reasonable that the NCI would study this approach in humans. Limiting the intake of fat to 20 percent of total calories in the diet may be difficult to achieve without fundamental changes in behavior toward food selection.

Even though governmentally funded efforts encourage healthy lifestyles and participation in prevention programs, the lack of individually perceived future value to be derived from personal investments has dampened enthusiasm for such programs (Comptroller General of the United States, 1985).

When a person feels well and is asked to risk denying himself some of life's pleasures for a gain that is both uncertain and in the discounted future, he will usually ignore the risk. Economists and health planners calculate the discounting in monetary terms; people feed the discounting in emotional and behavioral terms.

Critics blame our lack of success in motivating individuals to change from bad habits to healthy eating habits on traditional methods of providing nutrition education. The method tested here takes advantage of today's technology to provide nutrition education. The user will be able to track specific nutrient intakes easily and quickly without the need to keep burdensome records or spend more than nominal time with a counselor.

MOTIVATING BEHAVIOR CHANGE

Issues related to nutrition and food consumption involve complex interactions among social, cultural, economic and physiological factors. The application of behavior modification to induce lifestyle changes permits the shift of attention from defects within the person to the social environment around him. It is ideally suited to the analysis of just how social factors exert their influence.

Behavioral counseling can be traced back to several theorists; Pavlor, Skinner, Wolpe, Krumboltz, and Thoreson (Leitenberg, 1976). The theory of behavioral therapy states that people are born into this world in a neutral state. Environment, consisting of significant others (persons), and experience shapes their behavior.

In order to initiate behavioral change, one must understand the series of steps leading to change. First, one is exposed to a stimulus or piece of information. Then an understanding of the stimulus is obtained. Consequently, a change of attitude may result, which then may cause a change in action to occur (Williams & Burnett, 1981).

There are multiple strategies for motivating behavior change: thought stopping, cognitive restructuring, reinforcement, extinction, tailoring, shaping, and contracting.

Thought stopping is useful in controlling unproductive or self-defeating thoughts and images by suppressing or eliminating these negative cognitions. Cognitive restructuring involves using coping thoughts to replace negative or self-defeating ones. There is a great deal of similarity between the assertive thoughts described by Rimm and Masters, which involve positive thoughts after the self-defeating ones are interrupted, and the thoughts proposed in cognitive restructuring (1974).

Reinforcement is a crucial strategy for motivating changes. B.F. Skinner is credited with producing most of the basic research on the influence of reinforcement on learning (Skinner, 1965). The management of reinforcement has been referred to as behavior modification. Research has shown that behavior modification is useful in eliminating inappropriate behaviors and in producing goal-directed responses (Cohen, 1964). An unwanted behavior persists because it is reinforced. When withdrawal or prevention of reinforcement occurs, extinction of the behavior follows.

Tailoring, another strategy designed to motivate change, refers to the process of fitting the behavior to the client's daily routine. It assumes that each individual has unique circumstances to which the therapy must be adapted (Sackett & Haynes, 1976). In shaping, a gradual building of skills necessary to change a behavior are developed. The client proceeds in steps to achieve the set criterion and gradually reaches full performance (Snetselaar, 1983).

The last strategy for motivating behavior change involves a written agreement between counselors and clients. Because the contract is in writing, it provides a hard-copy outline of expected performance and a formal commitment to the treatment (Leitenberg, 1976; Plant, 1974; Sackett & Haynes, 1976).

To become self-directed, an individual needs to process information and monitor, control and alter the consequences. Self-evaluation provides the conclusion and is a continuous processing of behavioral information.

Stewart (1978) lists six steps to promote learning and minimize failure:

1. Divide information into manageable steps arranged in sequence;
2. Arrange for the first step to be managed with little effort;
3. Once the steps so that the client is capable of attaining each one;
4. Attempt to make each step within the instructions small, but not so easy or trivial as to appear worthless;
5. Involve the client in planning changes; and
6. State each step within the instruction so that everyone knows what is expected and whether or not each step has been completed.

Use of Microcomputers in Behavior Therapy

The impact of microcomputers has stimulated much interest in behavior therapy research. They offer unlimited opportunities to improve and enhance learning (McMurray & Hoover, 1984; Williams & Burnett, 1981; Russo, 1984; Carew, Elvin, Yon & Alster, 1985). The overall response to them has been one of very great acceptance (Burnett, Raylor & Agraw, 1985; Kransey, 1986; Carew, Elvin, Yon & Alster, 1985; Ellis & Raines, 1981; Huntington, 1980; Calvin, Calvin & Lagowski, 1981).

As was stated previously, behavioral changes depend on self-monitoring to provide immediate feedback. Microcomputers have helped to make dietary modifications such as reducing fat intake, easier and quicker by providing such feedback (Ellis & Raines, 1982). Their compact size also makes them easy to transport, which further enhances their practicality for continual behavior monitoring.

It is thought that immediate feedback on goal attainment continuously triggers an individual's decision-making process. Immediate feedback thereby enables a person to choose at that time whether to improve, maintain, or ignore present behaviors. It gives an individual the freedom to make his/her own decisions without interference from outside stimuli. With immediate feedback, a person is in control. Under such circumstances, behavioral changes are more likely to occur than if feedback is delayed.

Research also suggests that knowledge is enhanced 75 percent when information is presented by an interactive tool, as compared to only 15 percent when more traditional "teaching tools" such as instructors, counselors, and written materials are utilized (Krasney, 1986). With this in mind, interactive microcomputers which allow users to self-monitor food intake and to obtain immediate feedback on goal attainment may prove to be a viable alternative to initiating dietary change. If an individual can input values of foods eaten, into a computer and readily obtain a running total of his/her nutrient intake, the rest of the day can be planned accordingly to meet desired goals. Until recently, such continuous attention to behavioral change has been clinically impractical and technologically impossible in "real-life settings."

THE INNOVATION RESEARCH PROJECT

In the fall of 1985, NCI funded the proposal to design, construct, and test a prototype calculator through a Phase I SBIR contract. The objective of this phase was to establish technical merit and feasibility of the research that might lead to a commercial product. The duration of the phase is six months.

The project proceeded according to the following timetable:

1. Approach selection/project definitions   1 week
2. Design prototype   2 weeks
3. Construct prototype   2 weeks
4. Test prototype   3 weeks
5. Review of project by NCI   3 weeks
6. Run prototype against test data   3 weeks
7. Field test prototype (N=50)   9 weeks
8. Analyze data; prepare report   4 weeks

Instrument conception, design, construction, and testing (Steps 1-4) were done at Capital Systems Group, Inc. (CSG) facilities. System design and data analyses were also accomplished at CSG. A detailed discussion of the steps involved follows:

1. Approach selection/project definitions

a. In a computer-assisted study, the estimator table containing protein data was reviewed (Gardner et al., 1985). Derived fat data was substituted for protein figures. Mean values for calories and fat for each food group were calculated from frequency data obtained from the United States Department of Agriculture (USDA), National Food Consumption Survey [(NFCS) NTIS Accession Number PB82 138504]. Standard serving size (SSS) for food items were equivalent to amounts designated by NFCS as medium size. The SSS were translated into standard household measures and were adjusted in amounts to match the calorie and fat content of the members of the group; for example, two donuts is equivalent to a piece of pie (Figure 1). The acceptability of preliminary food groupings was determined on the basis of the estimator's ability to calculate fat to within plus or minus 15 percent of computer derived analysis of 50 previously collected records. Those food groups that did not meet the plus or minus 15 percent requirement were adjusted as required. When revisions to the estimator's food groupings were complete, a software requirements statement was developed.

b.   Design criteria:

-   Ease of entering food group information
-   Ease of correcting keying errors
-   Simplicity of documentation.

2. Design prototype; key elements included:

a.   A numerical coding system for identifying food groups on the keyboard (designed and tested).

b.   Software programmed to accept information concerning amounts of food consumed, keep a daily running total of nutrient values, store subtotals for access at next entry, store up to twenty-one day's

FIGURE 1
FOOD GROUPS AND STANDARD SERVING SIZES

Group #	Food Group	Standard Serving Size (SSS)
1	Whole milk	1 cup
2	Lowfat milk	1 cup
3	Yogurt	1 cup
4	Milk desserts	1 cup
5	Cheese, cheese dishes	2 oz, 1/2 cup
6	Meat	3 oz
7	Poultry	3 oz
8	Fish, shellfish	3 oz
9	Luncheon meats	1 oz
10	Eggs	1
11	Soups, tomato sauce	3/4 cup
12	Gravies	2 tbsp
13	Cream sauces	2 tbsp
14	Butter,margarine, oil mayonnaise; bacon	1 tbsp; 3 sli
15	Salad dressing	2 tbsp
16	Heavy cream, cream cheese, sour cream	1 tbsp
	light cream, coffee creamer	1 tbsp
	olives	5
17	Nuts, peanut butter, seeds	20, 1 tbsp, 2 tbsp
18	Legumes	1/2 cup
19	RTE cereals, breads, rolls, crackers	3/4 cup, 1 sli
	rolls, crackers	1/2, 3
20	Cooked cereals, pasta, rice	1/2 cup
21	Dark green or yellow vegetables and fruits	1/2 cup, med size
22	Potatoes and other vegetables	1/2 cup
23	Sweetened fruits	1/2 cup
	raisins, dried fruit	4 tbsp, 5 halves
24	Fresh fruit, fruit juices	med size, 1/2 cup
25	Mixed protein dishes, pizza,	1/2 cup, 2 small sli
	tacos, sandwiches, burgers	1
26	Sweetened and carbonated drinks	1 cup
27	Sugar, jam, jelly, syrup	2 tsp
28	Candy, cookies, brownies	1/2 oz, 2, 1
29	Cakes, pies	1 sli
	donuts, cupcakes, sweet rolls	2
	pastries	1
30	Potato chips, corn chips	10 med, 20
31	Popcorn, pretzels	1 cup, 40 sm
32	Beer	12 oz
33	Wine	4 oz
34	Liquor	1-1/2 oz

information to permit calculation of averages per day, and facilitate editing errors without rebooting programs and reentering data.

    c. Testing of software; revising when necessary.

3. Construct a prototype. To eliminate the possibility that the user could somehow write over (erase) the programs, or otherwise render the system inoperable, the unused keys were removed from the keypad and a small piece of plastic was inserted and glued into the power switch to prevent user entry into the programming mode.

    The software was designed to calculate a daily running total for calories and percent calories from fat, and to accumulate up to seven daily records for a weekly average. Edit features included the ability to go back to a previous day, add forgotten items, or subtract incorrect entries.

    For evaluation purposes, a program module was included to capture these data for subsequent comparison with subjects' written records. A sample of these record files is presented at the end of this document. Using sample dietary intake information, user guidelines and documentation to accompany the prototype were developed. Both guidelines and documentation were kept as uncomplicated as possible to encourage use by participants. A 3" x 5" instruction booklet was developed to use with the system.

4. Upon completion of the loading of the program into the computers, the food list and quantitatives were reviewed to determine their ability to produce nutrient estimates similar to those obtained by 24 hour recalls analyzed by a mainframe computer system. Diet records previously obtained from 50 subjects were coded by a trained coder, using the respondent's reported portion sizes and a detailed NFSC data base (NTIS Accession Number PB82-138504).

    These same diet records were then recoded using the "Estimate-it" data base, as if the respondents had used it to input their intake over a 24 hour period. Data analysis was done to determine whether estimates were within project specifications. This comparison of the calorie and fat values permitted the evaluation of three major potential sources of error inherent in the use of the computer. These included: the adequacy of the food groupings, the nutrient values applied to each food grouping, and the definitions of portion sizes assigned for each food grouping.

In order to evaluate the calculator performance and the instruction booklets, fifteen individuals were recruited, inhouse, to use the system for one week. Comments and suggestions were incorporated into both the program and the instruction booklet prior to distributing the prototypes for field testing.

5. Concurrently with steps three and four, the Principal Investigator meet with NCI Project Officers to review project plans and time lines. A sample study population was identified from the Lombardi Cancer Center and letters of intent obtained.

6. Upon completion of the above activities, the Principal Investigator designed a training plan, a quality assurance plan, and quality control procedures. These were discussed with project staff and site representatives prior to their institution. Calculators were distributed to the Lomabrdi population of 50 subjects currently collecting detailed dietary records. Each subject used the prototype for a period of two weeks. An evaluation was made in terms of user acceptance, ease of test use and potential value for education and training. To this end, both quantitative and qualitative information was collected through survey and feedback questionnaires. Focus group interviews were conducted to gather opinions concerning the value of this instrument in self-help programs.

Using an informal process, groups of from 4 to 8 subjects were encouraged to express their feelings and frustrations concerning the use of the computer prototype in any way they desired. All sessions were recorded and later transcribed. The moderator used the questions found in Figure 2 to keep the discussion focused on the topic.

In order to obtain some insight into user attitude toward the hand-held calculator by the study population as a whole, a questionnaire utilizing a Likert-type scale was constructed and administered (Figure 3). The Likert-type scale is a summated scale consisting of a series of items to which the subject responds. The respondent indicates agreement or disagreement with each item on an intensity scale. This scale is highly reliable when it comes to a rough ordering of people with regard to a particular attitude or attitude complex. The score includes a measure on intensity as expressed on each statement (Miller, 1978).

RESULTS

A standardized system for estimating daily dietary intake of calories and percent fat calories was successfully developed under the Phase I research. The product was given the name "Estimate-it" and a logo was designed.

Figure 4 graphically displays a comparison of dietary analysis data obtained from the hand-held calculator with that obtained from an IBM mainframe computer. No significant differences in either calories or grams of fat (P=0.9642 and P=0.8236) were noted. Of the 50 observations, two fell outside the plus-or-minus 15 percent range for calories and 8 were greater than the acceptable range for grams of fat.

Table 1 compares the hand-held calculator data with that obtained using an microcomputer-based nutrient analysis system. The results of a paired t-test showed no significant differences in total calories per day or percent fat calories per day either with the test diaries (P=0.9642 and P=0.8248) or the subjects' diaries (P=0.855 and P=0.2348).

The summary of focus group comments provides subjective data concerning user perceived benefits derived from use of the hand-held calculator. Comments frequently expressed a perceived benefit from

FIGURE 2
FOCUS GROUP DISCUSSION QUESTIONS

1. What did you think the main purpose of this trial was?

2. What did you want to gain from participating in this trial? Did this trial meet any of your expectations?

3. Did you find anything unclear or confusing about the instructional booklet? How might you improve it?

4. Did you find the calculator useful? How did you use the information it provided?

5. Did you learn a lot from the calculator that you did not already know?

6. If you could buy this calculator, how much would you pay for it?

FIGURE 3
QUESTIONNAIRE

The staffs of the Lombardi Cancer Center and Capital Systems Group, Inc. want to ensure that the "ESTIMATE IT" calculator is meeting the needs of individuals interested in modifying their eating behavior. We would appreciate your comments on the following statements, i.e., whether you agree or disagree with the items as they are stand.

Please check the appropriate blank:
----A(Strongly agree)
----a(Agree)
----U(Uncertain)
----d(Disagree)
----D(Strongly disagree)

1. This calculator is designed to give information about fat calories in groups of foods that are similar to each other.
    ___A ___a ___U ___d ___D

2. The instruction booklet contained more than enough information to use the calculator.
    ___A ___a ___U ___d ___D

3. The calculator was convenient to use.
    ___A ___a ___U ___d ___D

4. I was able to use the information given by the calculator to make changes in what I ate.
    ___A ___a ___U ___d ___D

5. The calculator helped me to decide what and how much of my favorite foods to eat in order to keep my fat intake down.
    ___A ___a ___U ___d ___D

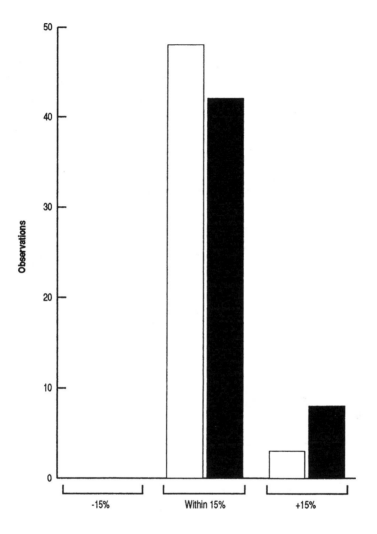

Figure 4. Comparison of Calculator and Mainframe Calculations.

Table 1
*Comparison of single purpose calculator data and microcomputer
data for total calories and grams of fat.*

Variable	n	Mean	Std Deviation	t-value	P-value
Evaluation Step 1					
Test diary calories	50	1.80	184.81	0.05	0.9624
Test diary Gms fat	50	0.44	13.88	0.22	0.8236
Evaluation Step 2					
Subject entered calories	68	49.85	235.55	1.75	0.0855
Subject entered Gms fat	68	32.87	226.07	1.20	0.2348

immediate feedback of information. Most subjects reported that the calculator had made them more knowledgeable about their diet and had helped them make changes in their usual eating patterns. They saw these changes as positive, helpful and healthful. Many commented that this technique made it easier, quicker and more interesting for them to evaluate their diets as compared to previously practiced methods, e.g., keeping written food diaries and the looking up of nutrient figures in a book. A few wanted to use the calculator for more than the allotted two weeks, and many asked if they could participate in the next phase to help further test the product (Figure 5).

FIGURE 5
SUMMARY OF COMMENTS

Group 1

"Although it's work, you get much more precise results than just writing it down and looking it up."

"I know cheese is high in fat,...but when I actually saw how many calories it was, and punching (those figures) in day after day, that really affected by habits. It was like..no more cheese!" I found myself cutting down on cream cheese and things like that."

"It is true, when you eat a cheese sandwich...you have had your (fat) count for the day."

"With the cheese, I think I learned like you did, This little computer (made me realize the amount of fat in foods). It was like ringing bells saying "You can't do that! ...I don't think low fat swiss cheese really makes that much of a difference."

(After I saw the figures for eggnog,) " I thought, well, I'll never drink eggnog again."

"When I actually saw the amount of fat in potato chips, I cut them out. I didn't put butter on bread... So I think I have done fairly well (to cut down on fat) except for cheese. I think having something like this is a marvelous tool. I love it...."

"Me too, I think you can change a lot of people's habits...my husband wanted to (use) it. " I said don't you touch it!"

"I wanted to go back (to the previous days) to see if I improved. I had problems with this. There might be something you might want to put in there to actually show you that you are going back."

(Q) "Did you find it bulky to carry around?" (A) "No."

"There is no redeeming social value to potato chips."

"(Q) "Any problem with fitting foods into one of the 35 groups?" (A) "Not particularly."

"You should have diagrams to get an idea how many ounces (meats) are."

Group 2

"Over the holidays I found myself...counting nuts. It really does start changing your habits and making you more aware."

"I have found that since I have cut my fat down, that if I eat high-fat foods, I can really taste it."

Summary of Comments continued

(Q)"Is any one sorry they participated (in this study)?" (A) "No, oh no. Do we get first on the list for prototypes?"

"....the process of "yes" or "no" and "is this the day" or "is this not the date," drove me nuts,...these food groups are not in any kind of order."

"I am a perfect example of a person who is not a bit interested in this type of thing (computer). I loved it. I really liked it. I want to buy one! I think it's wonderful! It helped me a lot to control what I eat."

"Some things are not on list, such as caviar."

"It's not "fair" not to count raw vegetables. If I have a salad with a small piece of cheese and 1 tablespoon of dressing, almost 100 percent of my calories come from fat."

"...I found this to be very helpful in "guiding" my diet. As the week went on, I found myself trying to cut down on the amount of fat. It would be nice if the calculator would display carbohydrates and protein for the day. It was fun doing the study."

Group 3

"It's difficult to keep track of what you eat at parties when you "nibble"."

"Some basics should be added, e.g., tuna salad, chicken salad."

"One has the tendency to overeat to compensate. If my percent fat was high, I had a beer to compensate. Perhaps we should know the "number of grams of fat" per day instead of "percent." Surely, if I eat nothing but vegetables and have a small piece of cheese, although my percent is high I couldn't possibly have eaten too much fat."

"I thought it was wonderful it you want to use it to help you lose weight. I'd be willing to pay $30 for it. I'd be delighted to pay a whole lot less (laugh)."

"It's like every other habit. When you do it many times, then you become familiar with it. It then becomes very easy and I think it works very well."

"It was complicated to go back to the previous day."

"So, I hope you let us know when it comes on the market. I usually get overenthusiastic when I like something."

Figure 6 graphically displays responses to the questionnaire designed to evaluate perceived benefits derived from using the Estimate-it calculator. Twenty-eight subjects returned the questionnaire. These questionnaires were scored in such a way that a response indicative of the most favorable attitude was given the highest score. Each individuals' total score was computed by summing each item score. The responses were analyzed to determine how scores reflect a given pattern of responses. Of the 28 individuals, two appeared uncertain as to the benefits of the computer; the remaining twenty-six appeared to perceive a benefit to be derived through the use of this product. Table 2 shows the distribution of the scores for each of the nine questions.

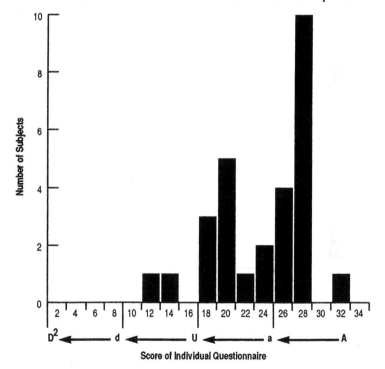

[1]N=28

[2]D=Strongly disagree; d=Disagree; U=Uncertain; a=Agree; A=Strongly agree

Figure 6. Distribution of Subjects[1] Perceived Benefit from Utilizing the Hand-Held Computer to Track Calorie and Fat Intake.

Table 2
Distribution of responses by twenty-eight respondents by individual questions from the questionnaire.

	Responses				
Question	A[1]	a[2]	U[3]	d[4]	D[5]
1	12	11	0	1	0
2	12	3	4	4	2
3	10	8	-	3	2
4	14	5	4	1	0
5	12	8	2	2	0
6	--	3	3	17	1
7	13	9	2	0	0
8	12	6	3	3	0
9	1($10);	1($15);	8($20);	6($25);	6($30); 2($35)

[1]A = Strongly agree
[2]a = Agree
[3]U = Uncertain
[4]d = Disagree
[5]D = Strongly disagree

Most respondents agreed that the computer was a useful and educational tool. Almost all indicated it took more than a week of use to build up sufficient familiarity with the calorie and fat content of the food groups to evaluate their dietary intake mentally.

POTENTIAL COMMERCIAL APPLICATION

Simultaneously with the preparation for the Phase II proposal, a business plan was developed and a market survey was conducted. Submission of these data to two venture capital organizations yielded a preliminary interest in supporting a Phase III effort. Market survey results and the business plan are included at the end of this case history.

NCI also expressed an interest in providing 30,000 individuals involved in an NCI sponsored woman's health trial these calculators to assist them in attempting to modify dietary intake to reduce fat in the diet. Given the publicity generated through these large scale government efforts, many individuals generally interested in improving their health through diet would be interested in tracking their own intake. A small, easy to use, easy to carry and affordable calculator designed for this purpose, would have a large potential market.

DISCUSSION

A prototype single purpose calculator utilizing a hand-held microcomputer was developed to examine the feasibility of providing on-line behavioral counseling to accomplish dietary modification. Strategies of behavior change, such as immediate feedback on goal attainment and response-contingent positive reinforcement, were incorporated. The effectiveness of such behavior-change procedures has been well documented (Rimm & Masters, 1974; Leitenberg, 1976). The six steps to promote learning and minimize failure suggested by Steward (1978) were also incorporated, enabling the user to become self-directed and able to process information and monitor, control and alter the consequences.

The calculator utilizes a numeric keypad and three function keys for respondent input and a character screen for displaying messages to the subject. The system also has an interface capable of downloading collected data for analysis.

Focus groups were used to obtain user input. The primary purpose of these groups were to "flag" areas in which the calculator could be improved and to obtain information concerning the subjects' attitude toward information supplied. The reaction of the study participants to the calculator was overwhelmingly positive. The most frequently reported comments centered around creating awareness and the general merits of receiving immediate feedback.

The prototypes were demonstrated to several site-review committees and to NCI Program Office. There was overwhelming enthusiasm for the product and a recommendation that it be incorporated into an ongoing women's health trial with an anticipated study population of 30,000.

OUTLOOK

The Phase II proposal was prepared and submitted in May, 1986. On February 10, 1987, a latter was received from NCI regarding the disposition of the project. Unfortunately, this approved project fell victim of budget reductions. NCI efforts to fund the Phase II production as an exception were also unsuccessful.

Unexpected support was obtained from an oncologist at the University of California, Los Angeles, currently involved in nutrition research. Seed money is being used to hand craft 50 production calculators independent of federal government support.

IMPLICATIONS OF THE CASE

This need oriented, potential innovation, fell victim to federal budget cuts. Indications are that the evolution of this product will, of necessity, be accomplished without government financing.

While the development requires a relatively modest investment, management has made the decision to permit the government to re-evaluate the project at the next review cycle some time in September.

References

Belloc, N.B., & Breslow, Y. (1972). The relation of physical health status and health practices. *Preventive Medicine, 1,* 409-421.

Burnett, K.E., Taylor, C.B., & Agraw, W.S. (1985). Ambulatory computer-assisted therapy for obesity: A new frontier for behavior therapy. *Journal of Consulting and Clinical Psychology, 53,* 698-703.

Carew, L.B., Elvin, E.W., Yon, B.A., & Alster, F.A. (1985). Using computer-assisted instruction to teach nutrition. *The Physiologist, 28,* 425-427.

Calvin, C.S., Calvin, E.W., & Lagowski, J.J. (1981). The effect of computer-assisted instruction on the attitudes of college students toward computers and chemistry. *Journal of Research in Science Teaching, 18,* 329-333.

Cohen, A.F. (1964). *Attitude Change and Social Influence.* New York: Basic Books. pp 124-140.

Comptroller General of the United States. (1985, September 30). *Constraining National Health Care Expenditures: Achieving Quality Care of an Affordable Cost.* Washington, D.C: Government Printing Office.

Dawber, T.R., Meadors, G.F., & Moore, F.E. (1951). epidemiological approach to heart disease: The Framingham Study. *American Journal of Public Health, 41,* 279-286.

Dawber, T.R., Moore, F.E., & Mann, G.V. (1957). Coronary heart disease: The Framingham Study. *American Journal of Public Health, 47,* 4-24.

Dawber, T.R., & Kannel, W.B. (1958). An epidemiologic study of heart disease: The Framingham Study. *Nutrition Reviews, 16,* 1-4.

Department of Health, Education, and Welfare. (1979). *Healthy People: The surgeon General's Report on Health Promotion and*

Disease Prevention. (DHEW PHS 79-55071). Washington, DC: Government Printing Office.

Ellis, L.B.M., & Raines, J.R. (1981). Health education using microcomputers: Initial acceptability. *Preventive Medicine, 10,* 77-84.

Ellis, L.B.M., & Raines, J.R. (1982). Health education using microcomputers: One year in the clinic. *Preventive Medicine, 11,* 212-224.

Farquhar, J.W., Maccohy, N., Woods, P.D., Alexander, J.K., Brestrose, H., Brown, B.W., Haskell, W.L., McAlister, A.L., Meyer, A.J., Nash, N.D., & Stern, M.P. (1977). Community educator for cardiovascular health. *Lancet, 1,* 1192-1195.

Ferguson, J.M. (1976). *Habits Not Diets.* Palo Alto, Ca: Bull Publishing Co. pp-31-32.

Fortmann, S.P., Williams, P.T., Hulley, S.B., Haskell, WlL., & Farguhar, J.W. (1981). Effect of health education on dietary behavior: The Stanford three community study. *American Journal of Clinical Nutrition, 34,* 2030-2038.

Gardner, L.B., Nixon, D.W., Gannon, J., O'Malley, D.T., Ellenberg, S.S., Besser, P.M., Mitchell, S., Paul, I., Carty, C., Hoffman, F.A., & DeWys, W.D. (1985). Assessing 24-hour dietary intake with a calorie/protein estimator. *Journal of Nutrition, Growth and Cancer, 2,* 219-228.

Huntington, J.F. (1980). Microcomputers and university teaching. Improving college and university teaching. *Journal of Nutrition Education, 24,* 75-79.

Kannel, W.B., & Gordon, T. (1969). *The Framingham Study: An epidemiological investigation of cardiovascular diseases.* National Institutes of Health: Bethesda, MD.

Krasney, S. (1986). Health care costs: The interactive solution. *Healthcare Computing and Communications.* pp 16-18.

Leitenberg, J. (ed.). (1976). *Handbook of Behavior Modification and Behavior Therapy.* Englewood Cliffs, NJ: Prentice-Hall. pp 440-441.

Maccohy, N., Farquhar, J.W., Wood, P.D., & Alexander, J. (1977). Reducing the risk of cardiovascular disease: Effects of a community-based campaign on knowledge and behavior. *Journal of Community Health, 3,* 100-114.

McMurray, P., & Hoover, L.W. (1984). The educational users of computers: Hardware, software and strategies. *Journal of Nutrition Education, 34,* 39-43.

McNutt, K. (1986). Avoiding the pitfalls of perfection: Resource allocation for the public good. *Journal of the American Dietetic Association, 86,* 186-190.

Miller, D.C. (1978). *Handbook of Research Design and Social Measurement.* (Third Ed.). New York: Longman. pp 73-89.

Multiple Risk Factor Intervention Trial Research Group. (1982). Multiple risk factor intervention trial. Risk factor changes and mortality results. *Journal of the American Medical Association, 248,* 1465-1477.

National Research Council. (1983). *Diet, Nutrition, and Cancer: Directions for Research.* Washington, DC: National Academy Press. p 104.

National Technological Information Service. NTIS Accession No. PB82 138504. Washington, DC.

Omenn, G.S., & Simopoulous, A.P. (1982). National nutrition policy in the United States. In: *Nutrition in the 1980's: Constraints on our Knowledge.* New York: Alan R. Liss, Inc. pp 473-479.

Omnibus Solicitation of the Public Health Services for Small Business Innovation Research (SBIR) Grant Applications. (1985). U.S. Public

Health Services, Department of Health and Human Services (PHS 86-1). pp 1-81.

Plant, R.F. (1974). Doctor's order and patient compliance (letter to the editor). *New England Journal of Medicine, 292,* 435.

Rimm, D.C., & Masters, J.C. (1974). *Behavior Therapy: Techniques and Empirical Findings.* New York: Academic Press. pp 416-449.

Russo, D.C. (1984). Computers as an adjunct to therapy and research in behavioral medicine. *Behavior Therapist, 7,* 99-102.

Sackett, D.L, & Haynes, R.B. (eds.). (1976). *Compliance with Therapeutic Regimens.* Baltimore: The Johns Hopkins University Press. pp 40-5.

Skinner, B.F. (1965). *Science and Human Behavior.* New York: The Free Press. pp 64-66.

Smith, S.W., Nelson, S.K., & O'Hara, J.J. (1982). *Final Report, Food for Thought Project.* Office of Policy, Planning, & Evaluation. Food & Nutrition Service, (Contract No. 58-3198-9-15). Alexandria, VA: U.S. Department of Agriculture.

Snetselaar, G. (1983). *Handbook of Behavior Modification and Behavior Therapy.* Englewood Cliffs, NJ: Prentice-Hall. pp 95-114.

Stamler, J. (1978). Lifestyles, major risk factors, proof and public policy. *Circulation, 58,* 3-19.

Stamler, J. (1982). Diet and coronary heart disease. *Biometrics, 37,* 95-114.

Stewart, N.R. (1978). *Systematic Counseling.* Englewood Cliffs, NJ: Prentice-Hall. pp 95-97.

Walker, W.J. (1977). Changing United States lifestyles and declining vascular mortality: Cause or coincidence [editorial]/ *New England Journal of Medicine, 297,* 1613-165.

Williams, C.S., & Burnett, C.W. (1981). Future applications of the microcomputer in dietetics. *Human Nutrition: Applied Nutrition, 38(A),* 99-109.

Yankelovich, Skelly & White, Inc. (1980). *Nutrition ms. Inflation. The Battle of the Eighties.* Washington, DC: Food Marketing Institute.

Appendix C

SUMMARY REPORT OF TECHNICAL REVIEW

AD HOC TECHNICAL REVIEW GROUP
April 30, 1985

SBIR Topic Number:	46
Title:	Development of Nutrition Education Materials, Including Software, Which Will Result in Long-Term Adherence to Diets Thought to Reduce Cancer Risk
Offeror:	Capital Systems Group, Incorporated Kensington, Maryland
Principal Investigator:	Ms. Lilly B. Gardner
Proposed Costs:	$49,908 (six months)
Period of Performance:	Six months

Recommendation:

Technical Merit:	Acceptable
Average Score:	700

SUMMARY OF REVIEW:

All 12 reviewers independently recommended that this proposal is TECHNICALLY ACCEPTABLE. The offeror appears to have the personnel, experience, facilities and capabilities to perform the work required successfully.

OBJECTIVES:

The offeror proposes to design a single purpose calculator to estimate (using food groups) calories and fat intake within 10-15% of actual intake per 24-hour period. The resulting prototype would be tested and its usefulness would be evaluated during the phase I period.

EVALUATION:

1. **Technical Approach:**

Strengths:

The proposal is written clearly. Methods and procedures appear to be logical and sound. The approach provides a quick feedback to facilitate user's decision making. A prototype would be developed, tested, and evaluated. The use of food groups is thought to eliminate the need for the user's ability to make substitution for items not listed in data base. The results as described are achievable. There is a need for a simple way to keep track of nutrient intake.

Weaknesses:

a. The approach does not address fiber at all.

b. The method proposed which was used to assess calorie/protein intake (which would be used also for calorie/fat) has not been published or validated. A trial using 50 subjects may not be adequate.

141

ғFICIAL ̱OFFIC̱L   OFFICIAL ̱OFFIC̱L ̱OFFICIAL

SBIR Topic No. 46
April 30, 1985 - Capital Systems Group, Incorporated

   c. The single-purpose calculator has very limited use and does not appear to
       be realistic. Although the estimation of calorie/fat is important, it is
       not clear how a business card calculator could be used for this applica-
       tion.

   d. The use of a nutrient estimator is thought to be unlikely to provide
       specific educational information about food content.

2. Personnel:

Strengths:

The proposed personnel have experience in developing nutrition related products,
and appear to be well qualified to perform the work required. The responsibilities and qualifications are clearly stated. The investigators include a
nutritionist, a health educator, and a programmer.

Weaknesses:

   a. The success of this project would depend on the availability of a com-
       puter chip for designing the computer. This may affect the phase II
       project.

3. Innovation and Potential Commercial Innovation:

Strengths:

The potential of developing a useful product appears to be very good. There is
a definite need for it. The idea to use food groups is thought to be technologically innovative.

Weaknesses:

   a. The approach is thought to need a lot of work to be successful commer-
       cially.

4. Facilities and Research Environment:

Strengths:

Adequate contact have been made for pilot tests. Equipment, software, and
facilities appear to be adequate to perform the work required.

Weaknesses:

None were noted.

OFFICIAL OFFICIAL OFFICIAL OFFICIAL OFFICIAL OFFICIAL OFFICIAL

Page 16 of 51

SUMMARY OF RATINGS
Ad Hoc Technical Review Group
April 30, 1985
SBIR Topic Number: 46

Proposal of:
Capital Systems Group, Incorporated (Single-Purpose Calculators)

Principal Investigator:
Ms. Lilly B. Gardner

Evaluation Criteria	Factor Weight	Reviewer												TOTAL SCORE
		No. 1	No. 2	No. 3	No. 4	No. 5	No. 6	No. 7	No. 8	No. 9	No. 10	No. 11	No. 12	
1. Technical Approach	40	240	320	320	280	280	200	240	200	240	240	320	360	3,240
2. Personnel	30	210	270	240	210	240	210	210	150	150	180	240	240	2,550
3. Innovation and Commercial Applications	20	100	180	180	120	160	140	140	120	120	60	180	160	1,660
4. Facilities & Research Environment	10	80	90	80	60	100	70	80	80	70	60	90	90	950
TOTAL	100	630	860	820	670	780	620	670	550	580	540	830	850	8,400
ACCEPTABLE (A)		A	A	A	A	A	A	A	A	A	A	A	A	
UNACCEPTABLE (U)														

Total Score: 8,400
Average Score: 700
Technically Acceptable: 12
Technically Unacceptable: 0

Appendix D

DEPARTMENT OF HEALTH & HUMAN SERVICES   Public Health Service

National Institutes of Health
National Cancer Institute
Bethesda, Maryland 20892

February 10, 1987

Reference: N43-CN-55517

Capital Systems Group, Inc.
1803 Research Boulevard
Rockville, Maryland 20850

Attention: James H. Kuhlman
            President

Dear Mr. Kuhlman:

The purpose of this correspondence is to bring you up to date on the status of your SBIR Phase II proposal and to advise you of our intentions with respect to your submission.

Before I address the specific issues, I would like to take this opportunity to extend, on behalf of the NCI, our apologies for the delay in this correspondence. While we would have liked to inform you earlier, several issues had to be resolved before we could do so. Among the issues we had to resolve were the budget and future SBIR awards. We anticipate that future informational correspondence will be more timely.

Based upon the peer and staff review, your proposal was deemed technically acceptable. However, based upon the funds available and the technical ranking of your proposal, you were not considered for award at this time. In the future, as funds become available, your proposal may be reconsidered for funding. This possibility is somewhat remote because it appears, based upon the response to the SBIR solicitations in grants and contracts, that there are more ideas than funds. However, we would like to keep all of our options open and propose that with your concurrence, we keep your proposal on file for reconsideration for the next seven months.

It is impossible at this time to reasonably predict with any accuracy the potential for funding. However, if you want your proposal retained and considered for possible funding at a future date, please so advise us by letter no later than March 9, 1987.

If your proposal is reconsidered for funding, there will be staff review to ascertain if the merit of the proposal is still valid. This review will be conducted prior to any funding decision and will consider such criteria as availability of the Principal Investigator, facilities, etc.

- 2 -

Should the situation be such that by September 1987 we can determine that the proposals will not be funded, we will advise you.

We appreciate your participation in this program and extend our most sincere apologies for our delay.

Sincerely,

Barbara Mercer
Contracting Officer
National Cancer Institute
Research Contracts Branch

cc: Lilly Gardner
     Principal Investigator

References

Aaron, H., & Schwartz, W. (1984). *The painful prescription: Rationing hospital care* (p. 113). Washington, DC: The Brookings Institution.

American Medical Association. (1984, October). *Professional liability in the '80s: Report 1* (pp. 3-16). Chicago, IL: American Medical Association.

Arthur Anderson and Company & American College of Hospital Administrators. (1984). *Health care in the 1980s: Trends and strategies* (p. 1). Washington, DC.

Atkinson, R. C., & Blanpied, W. S. (1985). Peer review and the public interest. *Issues in Science and Technology, 1*(4), 101-114.

Banta, H. D., Burns, A. K., & Behney, C. J. (1983). Policy implicataions of the diffusion and control of medical technology. *The Annals of the American Academy of Political and Social Science, 468,* 165-181.

Bartocha, B., & Solomon, T. (1985, February). Setting priorities for basic research. In B. Bartocha & S. Okamura (Eds.), *Transforming Scientific Ideas into Innovations: Science Policies in the United States and Japan.* Proceedings of the Third U.S.--Japan Science Policy Seminar (pp. 3-13). Tokyo, Japan: Japan Society for the Promotion of Science.

Battelle Institute. (1973). *Interactions of science and technology in the innovation process: Some case studies.* Washington, DC: National Science Foundation.

Belloc, N. B., & Breslow, Y. (1973). Relation of health practices and mortality. *Preventive Medicine, 2,* 67-81.

Blalock, A. B., & Blalock, Jr., H. M. (1982). Research design. *Introduction to social research* (2nd ed.). (pp. 59-90). Englewood Cliffs, NJ: Prentice-Hall, Inc.

Blendon, R. J. (1986). Health policy choices for the 1990s. *Issues in Science and Technology*, 2(4), 65-73.

Blumenthal, D., Gluck, M., Louis, K. S., Stato, M. A., & Wise, D. (1986). University-industry research relationships in biotechnology: Implications for the university. *Science*, 232, 1361-1366.

Booz-Allen & Hamilton. (1963). *Management of new products* (p. 9). Washington, DC: National Science Foundation.

Brook, R. H., & Lohr, K. N. (1986). Will we need to ration effective health care? *Issues in Science and Technology*, 3(1), 68-77.

Brown, C. G. (1985). The technological relevance of basic research. In B. Bartocha & S. Okamura (Eds.), *Transforming Scientific Ideas into Innovations: Science Policies in the United States and Japan.* Proceedings of the Third U.S.--Japan Science Policy Seminar (pp. 113-134). Tokyo, Japan: Japan Society for the Promotion of Science. Bureau of the Census. (1981). *Statistical abstract of the United States, 1981* (pp. 445-446). Washington, DC: U.S. Government Printing Office.

Califano, J. A., Jr. (1986). A corporate Rx for America: Managing runaway health costs. *Issues in Science and Technology*, 2(3), 81-90.

Campbell, D. T. (1979). "Degrees of freedom" and the case study. In T. D. Cook & C. S. Reichardt (Eds.), *Qualitative and Quantitative Methods in Evaluation Research* (pp. 49-67). Beverly Hills: Sage Publications.

Comptroller General of the United States. (1985, September 30). *Constraining national health care expenditures: Achieving quality care of an affordable cost* (pp. 4-15; 95-108). (GAO/HRD-85-105). Washington, DC: U.S. Government Printing Office.

Courtwright, D. T. (1980). Public health and public wealth: Social costs as a basis for restrictive policies. *Milbank Memorial Fund Quarterly/Health & Society*, 52, 268-282.

Crawford, R. (1977). You are dangerous to your health. *International Journal of Health Services*, 7, 663-680.

Cromwell, J., & Kanak, J. (1982, December). The effects of prospective reimbursement programs on hospital adoption and service sharing. *Health Care Financing Review*, 4(2), 67.

Cuca, J. M. (1983). NIH grant applications for clinical research: Reasons for poor ratings or disapproval. *Clinical Research*, 31, 453-461.

Denver Research Institute. (1976). *Why innovations falter and fail: A study of 200 cases* (R-75-04). Washington, DC: National Science Foundation.

Department of Health & Human Services. (1985). *Omnibus solicitation of the Public Health Service for Small Business Innovation Research (SBIR) contract applications* (pp. 1-36).

U.S. Public Health Service. Department of Health & Human Services. (1985). *Omnibus solicitation of the Public Health Service for Small Business Innovation Research (SBIR) grant applications* (pp. 1-81). U.S. Public Health Service.

Etzioni, A. (1978, May). Individual will and social conditions. *Annals of the American Academy of Political and Social Science*, 437, 62-73.

Farquhar, J. W., Maccohy, N., Woods, P. D., Alexander, J. K., Brestrose, H., Brown, B. W., Haskell, W. L., McAlister, A. L., Meyer, A. J., Nash, N. D., & Stern, M. P. (1977). Community educator for cardiovascular health. *Lancet*, 1, 1192-1195.

Felch, W. S. (1986, October). A pound of prevention...? [editorial]. *The Internist*, 27(9), 5-6.

Fortmann, S. P., Williams, P. T., Hulley, S. B., Haskell, W. L., & Farquhar, J. W. (1981). Effect of health education on dietary behavior: The Stanford three community study. *American Journal of Clinical Nutrition*, 34, 2030-2038.

Freund, D. A., & Jellinek, P. S. (1983). Financing and cost containment for personal health services in the 1980s. In S. C. Jain & J. E. Paul (Eds.), *Policy issues in personal health services* (pp. 43-44). Rockville, MD: Aspen Systems.

Freyman, J. G. (1975). Medicine's great schism: Prevention vs care: An historical interpretation. *Medical Care*, 13, 525-536.

Fuchs, V. (1976). *Who Shall Live?* New York: Pantheon.

Gellman, A. J. (1985, February). Incentives and disincentives to participate in the process of innovation: Some international speculations. In B. Bartocha & S. Okamura (Eds.), *Transforming Scientific Ideas into Innovations: Science Policies in the United States and Japan.* Proceedings of the Third U.S.--Japan Science Policy Seminar (pp. 183-197). Tokyo, Japan: Japan Society for the Promotion of Science.

Gibson, R. M., & Waldo, D. R. (1981, September). National health expenditures, 1980. *Health Care Financing Review*, 3, 1-54.

Goodstadt, M. S. (1986). Prevention strategies for drug abuse. *Issues in Science and Technology*, 3(2), 29-35.

Hanlon, J. J. (1974). *Public health: Administration and practice* (6th ed). (pp. 13-40). St. Louis: C. V. Mosby.

Illich, I. (1974). *Medical nemesis: The expropriation of health.* London: Calder and Byars.

Innovation Development Institute. (1986). Analyzing phase II conversion rates by agency and year. *InKnowVation*, 3(6-7), 9.

Institute of Medicine. (1983, November). *A Consortium for assessing medical technology* (pp. 1-2). Washington, DC: National Academy of Sciences.

Jacoby, I. (1983, December). Biomedical technology: Information dissemination and the NIH consensus development process. *Knowledge: Creation, Diffusion, Utilization*, 5(2), 245-261.

Jain, S. C. (1983). Policy concerns and the changing role of government in personal health: A perspective. In S. C. Jain & J. E. Paul (Eds.), *Policy issues in personal health services* (pp. 1-24). Rockville, MD: Aspen Systems.

Jaques, E. (1978). Complex organization and individual freedom. In E. Jaques (Ed.), *Health services: Their nature and organization, and the role of patients, doctors, nurses, and the complementary professions* (pp. 1-31). London: Heinemann.

Jonsen, A. R., Cooke, M., & Koenig, B. A. (1986). AIDS and ethics. *Issues in Science & Technology*, 2(2), 56-65.

Knowles, J. (1977). The responsibility of the individual. In J. Knowles (Ed.), *Doing better and feeling worse* (pp. 57-80). New York: W. W. Norton.

Lebow, J. (1974). Consumer assessment of the quality of medical care. *Medical Care*, 12, 328-337.

Levy, R. I. (1981). The decline in cardiovascular disease mortality. *Annual Review of Public Health*, 2, 49-58.

Logsdon, D. N., Rosen, M. A., & Demak, M. M. (1983). The INSURE project on life cycle preventive health services. Cost containment issues. *Inquiry*, 20, 121-126.

Logsdon, D. N. (1986). Should health insurance cover preventive services? *The Internist*, 27(9), 11-13.

Milio, N. (1981). The effects of policy on choice-making by health care consumers and practitioners. In *Promoting health through public policy* (pp. 91-113). Philadelphia: F. A. Davis.

Myers, S., & Marquis, D. G. (1969). *Successful industrial innovations* (National Science Foundation 69-17). Washington, DC: U.S. Government Printing Office.

National Academy of Sciences. (1978). *Systems for stimulating the development of fundamental research*. National Academy of Sciences. Washington, DC: U.S. Government Printing Office.

National Center for Health Statistics. (1983). National center for health statistics: Health--United States, 1982 (DHHS Pub. No. 83-1232). Washington, DC: U.S. Government Printing Office.

National Center for Health Statistics. (1984). *Vital statistics of the United States, 1980 life tables* (pp. 2; 16). Hyattsville, MD: U.S. Government Printing Office.

National Institutes of Health. (1986, December). *National Institutes of Health grants and awards*. Washington, DC: Grants Inquiries Office, NIH.

National Science Board. (1985). *Science indicators*. The 1985 report (p. 150). National Science Foundation. Washington, DC: U.S. Government Printing Office.

National Science Board. (1986). *Report of the NSB committee on excellence in science and engineering (NSB-85-50)*. National Science Foundation. Washington, DC: U.S. Government Printing Office.

Navarro, R. (1976). *Medicine under capitalism*. New York: Prodist.

NCI's SBIR awards move up in quality: Congress considers making it permanent; FASEB objects. (1986, September 19). *The Cancer Letter*. 12(36), 1-3.

NIH officials, skeptics debate at field hearing. (1987, December 14). *Federal Grants and Contracts Weekly*, pp. 1, 8.

Office of Technology Assessment. (1979). *A review of selected federal vaccine and immunization policies based on case studies of pneumoccal vaccine.* Washington, DC: U.S. Government Printing Office.

Office of Technology Assessment. (1982). *Strategies for medical technology assessment* (pp. 81-84). Washington, DC: U.S. Government Printing Office.

Office of Technology Assessment. (1984, July). *Medical technology and cost of the medicare program* (pp. 35; 81-84). Washington, DC: U.S. Government Printing Office.

Office of Technology Assessment. (1985, June, 30). *Technology and aging in America* (p. 164). Washington, DC: U. S. Government Printing Office.

Pratt, S. E., & Morris, J. K. (Eds.). (1984). *Pratt's guide to venture capital sources* *(8th ed.).* Wellesley Hills, MA: Venture Economics.

Public Law 97-219. (1982, July 22). *Small business innovation develompent act of 1982* (pp. 1-5). Division of Legislative Analysis, Office of the Director, National Institutes of Health. Washington, DC: U.S. Government Printing Office.

Robert Wood Foundation. (1982) *Annual report 1982* (p. 11). Princeton, NJ.

Roe, R. (1987). A technology policy study: Looking beyond "competitiviness". *Issues in Science and Technology*, 3(4), 12-13.

Roemer, M. I. (1984). The value of medical care for health promotion. *American Journal of Public Health*, 74, 243-248.

Rogers, P. J., Eaton, E. K., & Bruhn, J. G. (1981, May). Is health promotion cost effective? *Preventive Medicine*, 10, 324-339.

Rosenfeld, L. S. (1983). Regional organization and a national health program: A pipedream? In S. C. Jain & J. E. Paul (Eds.), *Policy issues in personal health services* (pp. 162-172). Rockville, MD: Aspen Systems.

Russell, L. B. (1984, September). *Evaluating preventive medical care as a health stragegy.* Final report of grant No. HSO 4392. (Available from the National Center for Health Services Research and Health Care Technology Assessment. Rockville, MD.)

Russell, L. B. (1986, October). Will prevention cut medical spending? *The Internist, 27,* 9,7-8, 10.

Ryan, W. (1971). *Blaming the victim.* New York: Vintage Books.

Schoderbek, C. G., Schoderbek, P. P., & Kefalas, A. G. (1980). Environmental scanning process. In *Management systems. Conceptual considerations* (pp. 193-226). Dallas, TX: Business Publications.

Schon, D. A. (1967). *Technology and Change.* New York: Dell Publishing.

Shapiro, H. T., Diebold, J., Gorton, S., & Massey, W. E. (1986). A national research strategy: Commentaries. *Issues in Science and Technology, 2*(3), 116-125.

Sirott, L., & Waitzkin, H. (1984). Holism and self-care: Can the individual succeed where society fails? V. W. Sidel & R. Sidel (Eds.). In *Reforming medicine: lessons of the last quarter century* (pp. 245-264). New York: Pantheon Books.

Sommers, A. R., & Sommers, H. M. (1977). *Health and health care, policies in perspective.* Germantown, MD: Aspen Systems.

Starr, P. (1982). The liberal years. *The social transformation of American medicine* (pp. 335-378). New York: Basic Books, Inc.

Tanon, C. P., & Rogers, E. M. (1975). Diffusion research methodology: Focus on health care organizations. In G. Gordon & G.

L. Fisher (Eds.), *The Diffusion of Medical Technology* (pp. 51-62). Cambridge, MA: Ballinger.

Teich, A. H. (Ed.). (1981). Reshaping technology. In *Technology and Man's Future* (3rd ed.). (pp. 412-418). New York: St. Martens Press.

Tesh, S. (1982). Political ideology and public health in the nineteenth century. *International Journal of Health Services*, 12(2), 321-342.

Thier, S. O. (1986). Health policy: The critical issues. *Issues in Science and Technology*, 2(3), 3-6.

Thompson, E. (1978). Smoking education programs, 1969-1976. *American Journal of Public Health*, 68(3), 250-257.

United States Congress. (1982). *Hearings before the subcommittee on Health and the Environment of the committee on Energy and Commerce of the House of Representatives*, 97th Congress (2nd Session on H.R. 4326, Serial No. 97-118). Washington, DC: U.S. Government Printing Office.

United States General Accounting Office Resources, Community, and Economic Development Division. (July, 1987). *Federal research. Small business innovation research participants give program high marks* (pp. 35-41; 42-46). (GAO/RCED-87-161 BR). Washington, DC: U.S. Government Printing Office.

United States General Accounting Office Resources, Community, and Economic Development Division. (March 1987). *U.S. science and engineering base, a synthesis of concerns about budget and policy development* (pp. 14-21). (GAO/RCED-87-65). Washington, DC: U.S. Government Printing Office.

United States General Accounting Office Resources, Community, and Economic Development Division. (October 25, 1985). *Implementing the small business innovation development act--The first 2 years* (pp. 7-31). (GAO-RCED-86-13). Washington, DC: U.S. Government Printing Office.

United States Public Health Service. (1978). Public Health Service scientific peer review regulations. *Federal Register*, 43, 7861-7866.

United States Public Health Service. (1979). *Healthy people: The Surgeon General's report on health promotion and disease prevention* (DHEW PHS 79-55071). Washington, DC: U.S. Government Printing Office.

United States Public Health Service. (1980). *Promoting health/preventing disease. Objectives for the nation* (DHHS PHS). Washington, DC: U.S. Government Printing Office.

United States Public Health Service. (1984). *National Institutes of Health*. Office of Medical Applications of Research. Washington, DC: U.S. Government Printing Office.

Vener, K. J. (1985). National Institutes of Health phase I small business innovation research applications: Fiscal year 1983 results. *Federation Proceedings*, 44, 2679-2684.

Westwood A. R. C., & Brupbacher, J. M. (1985). Putting science to work in a multi-industry corporation. *Transforming Scientific Ideas into Innovations: Science Policies in the United States and Japan*. Proceedings of the Third U.S.--Japan Science Policy Seminar (pp. 145-158). Tokyo, Japan: Japan Society for the Promotion of Science.

Wetzel, W. E. Jr. (1983, summer). An alternative to SBIR financing (pp. 37-39). *Sloan Management Review*.

Wilensky, G. (1984). Solving uncompensated hospital care: Targeting the indigent and uninsured. *Health Affairs*, 3(4), 54.

Yankauer, A. (1981). The ups and downs of prevention [editorial]. *Journal of Public Health*, 71, 6-9.

Index

157

National Cancer Institute
(NCI) v, 41, 47, 50,
51, 53, 54, 56, 67, 69,
84-86, 92, 113, 115,
119, 123, 134, 135
National Institutes of Health
(NIH) xi, 5, 9-11, 14,
16, 37, 40-42, 45, 44,
48-51, 53-55, 57, 59-
65, 67, 71, 75, 76,
89-95, 97, 99, 102,
104, 106, 107, 109,
112, 113, 136
National Science Foundation
(NSF) 12, 13, 35, 38,
40, 43, 65, 81
"new reductionism" 20
NIH, see National Institutes of
Health
NSF, See National Science
Foundation
Office of Medical Applications
Research 9-12, 16, 29,
94, 95
OMAR, See Office of Medical
Applications Research
Omnibus Solicitation 53, 62,
87, 147
patents 62, 80, 86
peer review 13, 15, 37, 40,
42, 45, 46, 49, 50, 53,
54, 57, 66, 69-71, 74,
77, 82-86, 92, 93, 99
Phase I 39, 45-47, 50, 51,
53-56, 67, 69, 70, 72,
73, 75, 76, 78, 81, 82,
83, 84, 88, 91, 92,
95-97, 103, 106, 109,
111, 119, 124

Phase II 39, 45, 47, 51, 53-56,
62, 67-69, 73, 75, 81,
82, 92, 95-97, 104,
106, 107, 109, 111,
132, 134
Phase III 39, 62, 104, 133
prevention xi, 6, 7, 9, 20, 21,
23-27, 31, 33, 34, 51,
70, 93, 95, 99, 115,
117, 136
PHS, See Public Health Service
primary disincentives 48, 64,
66, 68, 70, 73, 74
primary incentives 48, 59, 61,
70
priorities 12-15, 19, 90
Public Health Service 4, 5, 9,
103, 104, 136, 138
R&D, See Research and
Development
reimbursement policies 11, 27,
32-34
Requests for Applications
(RFA) 14, 50, 51, 67,
100
Requests for Proposals (RFP)
14, 50, 51, 100
Research and Development ix,
xi, 5, 9, 11, 12, 14-16,
32, 33, 37, 38, 39, 40-
43, 50-52, 57, 60, 62,
64, 67, 70, 72-74, 83,
87, 88, 90-92, 94, 96,
100, 104, 105
restrictions 15, 23, 96
RFA, See Request for
Applications
RFP, See Request for Proposals
rights in data xi, 62
SBA, See small business